The Family:

Money
Power & Respect

By
Fresh

ISBN: 978-0-9970227-2-8

Unique Literature Publications
417 Gulley St.
Goldsboro, NC 27530
(336) 709-2080

Editor: Taylor House Publishing
P.O. Box 720
Virginia Beach, VA 23451
taylorpublishinghouse@gmail.com
(757) 214-4926

Printed in the USA

Dedication

I want to dedicate this book to my kids. I do this and every other move in life with you guys in mind. Shout out to my kids' mothers for being excellent co-parents and staying drama free. I swear y'all make this easier. A special shout out to my parents...Mommy and Daddy, the real MVP's. Big ups to the whole King clan...Shout out to those guys in the belly...Without y'all's positive feedback and critiquing, this manuscript wouldn't be here. Last but not least...big ups to my city...Goldsboro, NC...My hood, Webbtown...My block Iraq...I hope everyone enjoys,

Fresh

Introduction

The Family: Money, Power, & Respect, is the first part of a trilogy. Travel with me as I take you through the gritty streets of Baltimore, Maryland and introduce you to a family who joins forces on different missions, but with one common goal in mind.

Bryce "King" Williams was once the king of Baltimore's drug trade until he was snitched out and sentenced to life in a federal penitentiary. After serving twenty years, he meets a big time lobbyist out of Washington D.C. who can guarantee King a full pardon out of prison. According to the lobbyist, our sitting President is in his last year in office and not above granting "personal" favors to those who helped him get his seat. Of course, the price of freedom is extremely expensive.

Determined to meet this goal, King enlists his family to help. Through another acquaintance, King learns that Baltimore is experiencing one of the worst droughts that the city has ever seen in its precious money maker, heroin. Thinking that the Gods are on his side, King takes advantage of the situation and arranges for a big shipment of heroin to be delivered from overseas by the son of a Chinese Triad Boss who is also in prison with King.

Fresh

The shipment arrives on schedule and King moves on to plan B of his mission.

King's son, Prince Williams, is an aspiring lawyer in his last year of college. Born and raised on Baltimore's Westside, Prince is far from a stranger to the streets. After a brush with the law that results in him getting kicked out of school, King approaches him with the opportunity to help free his father. After little thought, Prince agrees and teams up with his first cousin to help.

Prince's cousin, Raheem Phillips is in the streets. Faced with hard times from the current drought, he's overjoyed to be of assistance. The drugs that are provided, releases him from the reign of the current king of Baltimore and sets him on his own path of dominance.

Tyrell "T.O." Owens is the current king of Baltimore. He's sneaky, conniving and not to be trusted. He's also mastered the art of manipulation over the years. After having the streets snatched from under him by his protégé, he sets off a string of events to not only teach his protégé a lesson, but also bring him to his knees.

Princess Williams is Prince's twin sister. She is your average spoiled fly chick who enjoys partying, shopping, and having fun. It isn't until she finds out that her father has a chance of coming home that she gets serious about life and offers her two cents.

Gloria Phillips is the glue that holds this family together. The partner of one of Baltimore's biggest law firms, she has the connections and prestige to make things happen and she'll lay it all on the line for her family.

This book touches on various aspects of life other than the drug game and is written in the form of a mind boggling puzzle that will be crafted into a masterpiece. This first book addresses the money aspect of the family and how they amassed their fortune. The second installment, which I am hard at work on, touches on the power aspect of the family. Besides this manuscript, I also have other completed novels. I am proud to say that I take my craft very serious and have a vigorous work ethic. If you're looking for an up and coming author, I am your man.

Enjoy!!

Fresh

Chapter 1

(Raheem)

"Fuck," I screamed, while looking at Diamond with disgust. Not only had she just almost rear ended an Escalade, she also made me spill some of the chili from the burger that I was enjoying on my new Coogi shirt. "Watch where the fuck you going!"

"I'm sorry...Okay, I'm sorry." She shrieked while waving her hands in the air. "Damn, why do you have to scream and curse at me? You make me more nervous when you do that!"

I started to retaliate but thought better of it. Shorty was right. I had been doing a lot of unnecessary screaming and arguing lately. It wasn't her fault that shit is fucked up on the streets of Baltimore. It's election year. Our country is billions of dollars in debt. Wall Street is in chaos. Companies need bailing out and our sitting President don't give a fuck. The streets are on fire and my city is experiencing its worse drought ever in our prized cash crop, heroin.

My mind stayed in a thousand places at once. I can understand my girl's frustration. Point blank, she was a bad broad and used to the finer things. Money is funny my way though. I haven't had a decent pack since early February and it's now the end of May. Emotions are definitely running high in my household. I'm just not used to this shit. To me, it's like pandemonium and the world is slowly trying to cave in on a nigga. My phone rang and took me away from my thoughts.

"Who this," I asked while sipping on my tea.

"It's your cousin. What's poppin?"

I instantly sat up in my seat. Prince Williams is not only my first cousin, but he's also my best friend. My mother and his mother are sisters. I was hyped to hear from him though. He had called last night and spoke to me about a possible solution to all my problems.

"Same shit; another day, you got some good news for a nigga," I asked.

"I might do," he answered while coughing into the receiver. "I spoke to yo a minute ago. He screaming shit fucked up his way too, but his peoples maybe can put their hands on something."

"That's what's good," I answered, thinking that this was music to my ears. Yo that he referred to was a Mexican that he had linked up with who could possibly become a connection. I asked him, what types of prices did the dude have? He whistled before he answered and told me that the numbers were high, but workable. I was all ears.

* * * * *

(T.O.)

"And that my friend is why he is going to win this election," I said as I grabbed the remote and switched off the TV.

"Pac said it best when he said that we weren't ready for a back President." My right hand and loyal friend, Bruh explained. "There is no way that those crackers on Capitol hill is gonna allow a black man into their white house."

He went on to explain his point, but I wasn't listening. My mind was made up. I was so sure that the country was heading for a change that I offered to put a little wager. He looked at me in confusion at the request. Knowing that I'm not a gambler, he couldn't believe that I was even talking about a bet.

Before he could respond, I stood up. We were at my dealership, T.O.'s Autos, discussing the future presidential candidacy. Out of my peripheral, I spotted one of my lieutenants pulling up and prepared to greet him.

"What it look like, Rah? Don't tell me that Diamond has talked you into one of these fine vehicles that I have here," I said before dapping him and giving him and his girl a wink.

"Listen at you trying to make a dollar." Rah teased back, while leaning against his own car. "I came by to see what's really good."

Fresh

I leaned against his car for privacy. A nigga don't play the phones unless it's legit talk or pussy on the other end. Every little nigga on my team knew to come to either one of my establishments to talk business. I covered my mouth as if yawning when I did speak.

"It's still ugly. I thought I may have struck gold out west, but the El Salvadorians I was dealing with turned out to be hot."

"So what that means..." he started.

I nodded my head to confirm that I didn't know when the next package of heroin was coming in. He put his head on his chest as if he had lost his best friend.

Out of all the little niggas I dealt with, I liked this one the most. He didn't know it but me and his family had history. Besides that, yo is a go getter; loyal to the core. A little flossy, but what thousandaire in their twenties wasn't these days.

"I got plenty of that white girl, though. You're welcome to as much of that as you can handle," I offered.

He shook his head instantly. I nodded knowing where he was about to go. We had discussed this conversation enough. Plain and simple, the boy was used to dope money. Yo ran a million dollar a week dope shop for me over in West B-more. It would take a month or two for him to see the kind of money he brought in fucking with that coke. Isn't no money like dope money and he respects that. After a moment he spoke.

"I might know a little something," he whispered and scooted closer. "My cousin Prince is up in Pennsylvania at college. He got a line there with some Mexicans."

I was all ears as he explained that his cousin had managed to set up a deal with the amigos. According to him, they were willing to hold five kilos if he was willing to come get them ASAP. I immediately shook my head and stopped him. Five kilos wasn't enough product for me and he should know this. Hell, that was only enough to supply his block. I have customers lined up all over the east coast waiting for me to supply them. I explained that to him too.

"I wasn't suggesting that you cop the work," he informed. "I was asking if it was alright if I copped the work and let it go out of the shops."

It didn't take long for me to agree to that. He was basically responsible for the entire Westside. He had little niggas who were practically starving these last two months due to the drought. Niggas needed to eat. It was no way I could deprive the nigga of stepping out. And if this deal goes good, this could be the start of a new plug. If the amigos could touch five, then they might could touch a hundred.

Fresh

"I got no problem with that. You know you gonna have to grease those other palms," I stated, speaking of the police. Protection cost in the city.

"No doubt," he responded. "That is the least of my worries. My problem is that these amigos are taxing the fuck out of a nigga. They aren't slow. Those fuckers are asking for ninety a demonstration. Shit's been so fucked up lately that I'm a little short on the re-up."

I nodded, thinking that he was good for a loan. I asked him what he was short and when he told me, I whistled. Before I could comment, he cut me off.

"The shit probably some tar, but with some luck, I can hit it harder, flip that, and hit you with a little something extra for the favor. Everybody will eat."

I thought of his proposition, told him that the extras weren't needed and agreed to his terms. He needed to hit the highway ASAP. I told him to send his people back in an hour to pick up the money.

* * * * *

(Princess)

"I'm sorry miss, but this card has been cancelled," the saleslady in Macy's cosmetic department stated.

"Cancelled," I asked with an attitude.

My insides were on fire. This was the work of my bitch of a mother. She had threatened to do this last week, but I didn't think she would make good on her promise. The saleslady was talking some nonsense about calling customer service, but I wasn't listening. I quickly dug through my Vuitton wallet and handed her my American Express.

She swiped that card, waited a second and handed it back to me. I wanted to cry. I swore then and there that my mother would pay for this embarrassment. I glanced behind me. There was a line patiently waiting. The Mac products that I wanted came up to $197.34. I only had two crisp one hundred dollar bills. Not knowing how far my mother was gonna take this, I cringed and peeled off my last.

Products in hand, I dialed my mother's office while my eyes scanned the crowded mall for the nearest ATM. I spotted one and headed in that direction.

"Tolson, Brooks & Phillips Law Offices; this is Jenny speaking. How may I direct your call," the office receptionist answered.

"Hi Jenny, this is Princess," I announced in my sweetest voice while sliding my card through the slot. "Can you direct me straight to my mother?"

She told me that my mother was in court at the moment and wasn't expected to be back for the day. She asked did I want her voicemail.

Fresh

Hell no, I didn't want her voicemail, I said to myself while glancing at the screen in front of me. According to the bank, my balance was zero. Steam coming from my ears, I asked Jenny which courthouse I could find my mother at and headed for the parking lot.

My mind was everywhere and thoughts ran rampant. What type of shit was my mother into; cutting my cards off. Her recent complaint was that I didn't want or try to find a real job. What she failed to understand is that modeling is a real job. It's just not your average job. The competition is fierce out here. However, my agent has assured me that big plans are in the works for my future.

Outside in the parking lot, I couldn't find my brother's car. I own a new Lexus ES 300 myself, but my baby is in the shop due to a minor fender bender that occurred while coming from Ibiza the other night. Instead of letting me borrow one of her cars, she was punishing me by making me drive my brother's tricked out Magnum. It took me another ten minutes to locate the car because I didn't have his alarm chirper on my key chain. When I did finally find the whip, I quickly pointed his machine in the direction of the federal courthouse.

I found my mom in courtroom three, deep into a hearing. I knew it wasn't a trial because there wasn't a jury present. The judge was rambling off some legal mumbo jumbo to my mother while she dug through her files on the table. The prosecutor sat to her left with an obvious smirk on his face.

Mom was in trouble. I wanted to pinch her to add extra stress to her already rattled persona. Instead, I made my way to the front pew and made enough noise for her to look back. After rolling her eyes at me, she turned back to the judge.

"Your honor, I'm sure I have the case history in question because I printed it up myself. If I may ask the court to postpone this…"

Ten minutes later, we were both on the elevator in route to the ground floor. "The Bitch," as I sometimes called her behind her back, didn't give me any help so I started in on her.

"I was at the mall earlier and all my cards were turned off. Not only that, but my ATM balance is zero. How could you?"

"It was easy," she smirked as we climbed into her Benz. "I simply called American Express, Visa and the bank and told them to clip you. It was quite simple. Probably didn't take but fifteen minutes."

"But mom…" I started.

"Don't but me Princess. It's not gonna work this time. It's obvious you're taking my kindness for weakness. You're a spoiled, irresponsible and ungrateful little bitch," she added with a look that dared me to object.

Fresh

"You run through my money as if it grows on trees. Both of your cards have a $5000 dollar a month limit and they're both maxed every month. You don't even take your allowance money that I give you and pay your own bills. I know this because your bills always end up on my kitchen table every month. I buy you a car and you wreck the damn thing! I refuse to keep going on like this!"

"But..." I started again, but she held up a finger to silence me.

"I don't mind the money baby; honestly I don't. The least you could do is show a little gratitude. You don't do shit but shop, sleep and club every day. I ask you to take mama on her errands and you won't even do that. I ask you for simple shit like picking up my clothes from the cleaners and it never gets done. I'm like...Damn!" She paused and smiled as a US Marshall came within earshot. "It's like this Princess. Until you can bring something to the table, your ass is cut off. Don't ask me for shit!"

With that said she pulled out the underground garage and circled the block until she spotted Prince's car. After pulling beside it, she calmly lit a cigarette and waited for me to get out. I refused to budge though.

"So what am I supposed to do? I'm totally broke. B.R.O.K.E; broke. There is no food in my fridge or gas in my car," I said with desperation in my voice.

For an answer, she patted my face, told me I was beautiful and would come up with something.

* * * * *

(Prince)

The meeting spot was in Philadelphia. I caught the train down. Rah was due to meet me early the next morning. As soon as I arrived, I caught a gypsy to the nearest Marriot, checked in, ordered a pizza and crashed.

My phone woke me early in the morning. I saw who it was before I answered and made a joke about it being too early.

"Fuck that kid! This is business. Better early than late; where you at," was his response.

I rolled out of bed, found a hotel brochure and rambled off the address. He told me he would contact me as soon as he was downstairs. I yelled for him to stop for breakfast before hanging up. After relieving myself, I hopped in the shower. Twenty minutes later, I was letting Rah in. He rolled a blunt while I ate.

"So how is this supposed to go down?"

I told him that I had already made a call and left a message that we were ready on my man's machine. I explained that it was just a waiting game now. Rah lay back and lit his blunt. After taking a

Fresh

few hits, he passed it to me and reached for his phone. I heard him blow his girl Diamond a few kisses before hanging up.

"You trust these wetbacks? I mean, we are dealing with a lot of money here," Rah commented.

"Come on shorty…I wouldn't even have you involved if I didn't trust yo. Yo may be a wetback, but I can tell he's about his business. The nigga ride fly in a little supped up Acura joint. Yo blow nothing but the best like we do; sour diesel, haze and shit like that. He lives in a nice little townhouse off campus. The nigga don't got a job; said that his brother takes care of him. You know what that mean."

Rah was paying attention. It's no secret in most circles that amigos do their thing like most blacks. From what I was telling him, it didn't take a rocket scientist to know that I was dealing with a connected dude. He asked how I hooked up with yo. After accusing him of interrogating me, I reached for the blunt before I spoke.

"The cat be blowing. When he runs out, I sell him a little of my personal. That led to us blowing together. I peeped a few pictures of his brother and asked what the deal was. He told me he would get back at me. The rest is history. I knew he was really about his business when he put that steep price on the table," I told him.

Rah was convinced. I pulled out my PSP while he tried to get some sleep. My phone rang a little before noon. It was my peoples.

"Luis," I answered cheerfully.

"Que pasa? You in Philly?"

"Si! I'm in North Philly right now at the Marriot on University Drive," I informed him.

"I know where you're at. Stay by the phone and I'll call you shortly. Is everything straight on your end?"

"Everything is good this way. I'm just waiting on you so I can get the fuck out of dodge."

"Twenty minutes, mi amigo," he explained and hung up.

When he showed up, he appeared to be alone. As soon as he stepped in the room, he reached into his dip and produced one kilo. Rah quickly cut into the package, took one look and knew shit was legit.

Rah explained that it was the popular "tar" heroin before sitting it aside and heading to the car to get the money. Luis produced a blunt of his own and lit up. Rah came back shortly after that with a book bag. He dumped its contents out on the bed. Stacks of money and a money counter fell out. After plugging up the machine, he handed Luis nine stacks. The Mexican grinned, evidently liking what he saw.

Fresh

"Yo Prince, we got a problem man," Luis stated as he ran the first stack through the machine. "My brother is impatient, man. He sold the other four last night, baby. That one is all I have right now."

I gave him a disappointed look before getting into his ass. He was supposed to hold me down. I pointed to the money and asked did he think I was a joke or something. He held up his hands.

"I knew you were good man. It's my brother who wasn't convinced. At the same time, it's his shit...I did everything in my power to get him to hold them shits." He shrugged his shoulders and continued. "But check, he'll know shit is legit when he sees this money. As soon as he gets right again, I'll give you a call."

I looked at Rah who only nodded his head. I went into hustler mode and asked for a cheaper price since we were copping so much and coming to get it. He told me that he would mention the price reduction to his brother but he couldn't promise me anything.

We all left the hotel together ten minutes later. Rah was driving a new Chrysler Pacifica. He had the stash built in it and all. After securing the product, we hit the highway without even checking out properly. By the time we made it to Maryland, I needed to use the restroom. We found a little store off the first exit we saw.

"Get some Dutch's while you're in there," Rah yelled as I made my way into the store.

I gave him the finger and mouthed that he wasn't smoking any weed with that shit in the car; especially not while I was in there with that shit.

"Man, just get me a Dutch and be quiet," he whined.

After using the restroom, I copped two Gatorades and a box of cigars. Not bothering to get a bag, I scooped up my purchase and headed for the door.

A State Police was entering the store as I exited. He immediately glanced at the cigars in my hand and gave me a knowing look. Rah was laid back busting up buds when I got into the car. I cranked up instantly.

"Hold up yo…," he started, but I was pulling off already.

He showed me the bag of weed and pointed to the stash that was still open. I nodded my head in the direction of the police cruiser. The cop that I had nearly bumped into was now getting into the cruiser where his partner waited. He had his eyes on us too. I knew they were coming to fuck with us before they even got behind us.

Fresh

"Stuff that tree in your nuts and buckle up," I said as they hit their lights on us. "Just act normal. I got this."

I knew the drill before he asked for the paperwork and handed it over. He disappeared to his cruiser while his partner stood by to keep watch. I rolled Rah's window down.

"Excuse me officer, but why were we pulled?"

"Just be patient; my partner will explain everything when he returns." He spit a mouth full of chewing tobacco out. I knew then that we were in trouble.

"Fuck this shit yo! Pull off," Rah whispered to me.

That wouldn't have been a problem earlier. They had my license and everything now. There wasn't shit I could do. The other officer reached my door and asked me to step out.

"What seems to be the problem officer? Or better yet, why were we pulled over anyway," I asked while complying.

The officer took me to the back of the car and pointed to the tag. He told me they were slightly altered and that he couldn't read them clearly. I glanced at the tag. The car was a rental. Around the tag was a label that read "T.O's Auto" and listed a number. It was harmless and most rentals came with a label. Before I could protest, another cruiser pulled up. The K-9 dog had arrived.

"The reason I pulled you out of the car was because I can smell marijuana. Are there any drugs or weapons in the vehicle," he asked.

I knew the routine. Dude wanted me to panic or get loud so he could really have a reason to search the car. I made sure my tone of voice was in check before I replied.

"Officer, you are mistaken if you think you smell marijuana in that vehicle. I, nor does my passenger smoke. There are no drugs or weapons in the vehicle. The real reason you pulled me is…"

"I didn't ask you all that," he answered while getting a little red around the neck. He walked over and peeked into the vehicle. "Where are you coming from with that luggage?"

"I'm just a student from Penn State University. This is my cousin. He just picked me up for my summer vacation." I reached and produced my college ID.

He took that, examined it and then went to congregate with his buddies. After a minute, he asked if it was okay if he searched the vehicle. I politely declined. He stated that he was gonna run the dog around the car and if the dog alerted, then he would search. As soon as the dog got to the passenger door, it sat down.

Fresh

Chapter 2

(Gloria)

I woke up this morning with a funny feeling, when actually I should have been on cloud nine. My fiancé, Darius Wilcox, who had been in Atlanta at a broker's convention, surprised me yesterday with flowers, dinner and a night on the town. He concluded the night with some out of this world sex. Sex was so good that I was bypassing my morning ritual of a four mile jog around my exclusive Berry Downs estate.

After a luxurious cold shower, I met Darius in the kitchen. He had the table set for two. Blueberry muffins, a bowl of fruit and orange juice, were his breakfast of choice. He set the USA Today he was reading down and pulled me in close for a kiss.

"Umm... What was that for," I asked while grabbing a grape from his bowl.

"That was for G.P. Now this..." he said while offering his tongue. "This is for last night!"

I pulled away quickly. Anymore of that and I would be back upstairs getting a repeat performance of last night. He pinched my ass and barked like a dog as I escaped to the phone on the counter. My son Prince was supposed to arrive from college yesterday. For some reason, he hadn't contacted me, which was very unlike him. I asked Darius what he had planned for the day while I dialed Prince's number.

"I and the other Deacons have a meeting with the Bishop today to discuss the children summer camp program. I have to close on a condo in D.C. at three." He stretched and yawned. "After that, I was hoping you would join me at my house tonight so I can cook for you."

I could only grin. This guy was a ladies' dream come true. He was determined to turn a West Baltimore girl like myself into some kind of exotic Queen. Few people knew the truth about my past. He was one of the few.

Darius knew about my struggle. He knew how I did almost anything necessary to raise my two children by myself after their father was convicted of numerous charges and sentenced to life. Darius knew how I went from rags to riches after that conviction. He knew how I struggled through law school after completing the bar, made a name for myself that grew to attach three associates and two paralegals. He knew how my hard work and determination led me to be courted by my now full partners to join their team and how with me at their side, our firm grew to become one of the top law firms in Baltimore.

Tolson, Brooks & Phillips now boasted more than sixty-eight lawyers and over one-hundred paralegals. We practice every form of law; probate, tax, criminal and so forth. I head the criminal law division personally. Under me alone, I oversee twenty-six of the firm's sixty-eight lawyers. I net the firm a little over half of its yearly income. To put things in perspective, I'm a gold mine; a go getter, someone to be reckoned with. I am known to turn nothing into something. I'm what some will call the poster child for the phrase "Rags to Riches."

I accepted Darius' invitation for dinner, told him my schedule was light today and headed off to work. In my Benz, I tried Prince's number again and got the same result. That irritated me. I know it's wrong to show favoritism between my kids, but I must admit that I'm a little more biased towards my son.

Prince is laid back, a thinker, not afraid to listen but knows how to be heard when needed. My daughter, his twin sister, is the exact opposite. Shorty girl is more like her father. She wants the world and wants it now. Wanting the world is not a bad thing, except like her father, she has no intentions to work for it. I decided to leave a message this time.

"Hey baby, it's your mom. Call me ASAP. Sorry I missed you yesterday," I said before hanging up and dialing Princess' number next. She answered on the first ring.

"Hey, mommy; I was just about to call you!"

My antenna went up. She was too cheerful. Shorty was plotting for something, probably money. I asked had she heard from her brother.

"Shit…I forgot all about Prince was coming home." Her shock sounded genuine. "Which reminds me; what am I supposed to drive once he demands his car?"

To my surprise, she hadn't called whining since our fall out a couple of days ago. I wondered what she had been up to since then. Instead of asking, I issued a few instructions as a test.

"I guess you can use my truck for the time being, but I need you to run a couple of errands for me today."

She agreed and waited while I told her to pick my mother up at noon and take her grocery shopping. So happy to be getting my truck, she eagerly agreed. Before she hung up, I told her to keep her weekend free so we could all make the trip to see her father. As soon as I hung up the phone rang in my hand.

"You have a collect call from, 'Prince,' an inmate at the Cecil County Detention Center. To accept…"

My heart was beating a mile a minute. Why in the hell was my boy in jail and in Cecil County of all places? Everyone knew that little ass town was nicknamed 'Crackerville.' I waited patiently until the automated recording ended before pushing five.

"What are you doing in jail...," I started.

"I need you ma. Me and Rah are locked up together. They found..."

I cut him off before he incriminated himself. The jail phones are notoriously tapped and admissible in court.

"Whatever they found is not important. Just tell me what they have you charged with and what your bond is."

"We're charged with Trafficking a Controlled Substance. Our bond is a million dollars apiece. But, mama..."

I wouldn't let him continue. Instead, I told him that I would be there shortly to see what I could do. The lawyer in me kicked in and I started to issue out orders. I told him not to make any more calls from the jail and to relay the same message to his cousin. After drilling that into his head, I asked if they had made any statements to the officers. He confirmed that they hadn't and hung up.

Then, I called my office and gave a few instructions to my secretary.

"Laura, I'm not coming in today. Anything important on my docket, reschedule as you see fit.

Fresh

Call Randall Traynor down at Rifkin, Rifkin & Petelli and have him call me immediately. Tell him I'm calling in that favor. He'll know what to do."

She repeated all that I had just told her and hung up. I maneuvered my car onto the next exit to hit I-95 North. The million dollar bond clouded my thoughts. What in the hell had those boys gotten themselves into?

* * * * *

(T.O.)

My soon to be ex-wife Diane woke me up with the news. After seventeen years of marriage to an outrageous, cheating husband, she was ready to call it quits. I couldn't be mad. To tell the truth, I was surprised that someone as headstrong and intelligent as her had waited this long to leave.

The founding partner of her own accounting firm, she handled the money of many professional athletes and politicians that resided in the DMV area. My money wasn't all that motivated her to stick around. I must say that shorty is just an all-around good woman; and now that we are at the final stages of our divorce, I feel a little regret at losing her.

We still share the mansion in Owing Mills. Still sleep in the same bed. She occasionally will let me get the pussy. She still has a nigga's best interest

The Family: MONEY, Power, Respect

at heart; which was evident when she handed me the morning paper and pointed to an article.

"Two arrested in Cecil County...A kilo of pure heroin and over sixty thousand in cash confiscated..."

My eyes scanned the rest of the article which briefly summarized what happened and who was locked up. Showing no emotion, I tossed the paper to the side and headed to the restroom. When I returned, Diane handed me a cup of coffee.

"One of your boys," she asked with a raised eye. "I thought I recognized the Phillips' name."

She got up and prepared to leave the room. She asked if I would be joining her downstairs for breakfast or did I want it brought up. I told her that I wasn't hungry and reached for the phone. I called Bruh, who knew nothing of what went down. I told him to get our lawyers on the job, ASAP.

"I'm on it. Anything else," he asked.

"I guess you can try and get a message to old boy to be patient and that the bond is too big right now, but to not worry because we are on our job. He'll know what's up," I said as I finished my coffee.

"What about the other one. He's not one of us," Bruh commented.

I knew who Prince was, but didn't know him personally. I did, however, know his father and aunt real good. I also knew that his mother was a famous woman attorney who could beat almost any charge. Shorty had plenty of paper. Prince would be just fine. My main concern was Rah at the moment. He was the one who could implicate me in the case. With that in mind, I told him to just worry about Rah.

After hanging up, I read the article again while wondering what the hell went wrong. Was it a set up the whole time? And where the fuck was the other dope they were supposed to have?

Whatever the case, after this incident, I was gonna have to put some serious distance between myself and the boy Rah. Yo was sure to be hotter than a firecracker.

I started to formulate a plan in my head and smiled at my thoughts. His being locked up would give me the perfect opportunity to do something else I been wanted to do. Diamond sounded sleep when she answered.

"We have a problem. It's about Rah. We might need to meet. You know how I feel about these phones," I started.

* * * * *

(Prince)

I don't know what type of strings she pulled, but before three in the evening, they were calling my name to be released. I really hadn't been sweating the situation anyway. A million may be a steep bond, but my mom is worth that. It was Rah getting out that concerned me.

True indeed, Ma loved Rah like a son and would no doubt try to get him out; but a million dollar bond is a lot of money. If anything, he was bound to have to sit tight until she got his bond lowered.

Unlike me, Rah has a criminal record. He had a possession of a stolen vehicle case on his rap sheet. Whatever the case, he walked me to the gate with a few last minute instructions.

"Just go see yo, like I said. Explain to him what went down. Tell him I'll probably need his help on the bond. Other than that, I'll straighten everything out when I touch."

I nodded and explained that I would relay his message as soon as I touched the city limits. I still tried to keep his confidence up, though, and told him that mom was probably working on his bond as we spoke.

"Let's hope that she is," he grinned. "Oh yeah, swing by my crib and check on my Pooh. You know she not built for this type of shit. I'll bet you that she is about to go crazy right now."

We dapped it up one last time and I was out the door. Mom was waiting for me up front. She was in deep conversation on her cell. I hugged her neck and couldn't help but hear her mention Rah's name to whoever she was talking too. That alone put my mind at ease.

I handled my business with the commissioner and we were out the door. As soon as we were out of ear shot she told me that she had just spoke to Randall Traynor about Rah and that the highly respected defense attorney was on his way to see what he could do.

"If he can just get the bond down to 250 grand like I did yours, then Raheem will be out no later than tomorrow morning." We reached her car and she lit a cigarette. "Now tell me everything that went down and don't leave out shit!"

I told her the whole story from start to finish; leaving out nothing. My major is Pre-Law, so I'm pretty familiar with the law. I knew that the whole stop and search was illegal. The case could be beat.

My only regret was the money that it would cost to actually beat it. Her representation wouldn't cost me a dime, but it would tap into her funds. After I was finished explaining everything, she was on her third Newport. She lit another before she spoke.

"Everything should be okay if it went down like you say." She nodded and searched my eyes for the truth.

"Ma, it was a straight up fluke. Dude only pulled us because he saw those blunts in my hand. We hadn't been smoking or nothing," I assured.

"And neither of you made a statement," she asked again. I confirmed we hadn't. "The car was registered to someone else. The drugs and money were in a secret compartment. Hell, the car was a rental. That dope could belong to anyone; and if that doesn't work, I can probably challenge the dog alert and win."

I nodded and pointed out the getting the store surveillance tapes would surely prove how it all went down. She told me that she wanted the discovery before she formed a plan of action. After she saw what they had against us, then she would prepare accordingly.

We drove the rest of the way in silence. The county jail had worn a nigga out. I felt exhausted, but horny. Raheem wanted me to go see his connect today, but all that could wait until morning. At the moment, all I wanted was to see my daughter and baby's mother.

* * * * *

(Princess)

I was finished with Big Ma and her errands before the close of business hours. Old fashioned as ever, she didn't trust the internet to pay her bills. It took the whole day for us to pay each and every bill separately. After we finished with her grocery shopping, we headed uptown to cop her two nice church hats. We both got hungry after all that shopping, so she treated me to dinner at her favorite restaurant, Outback.

After dropping her off, I cruised through my old neighborhood. Nothing had changed. The dope boys still dominated the blocks while the fiends looked like zombies. A few of the niggas waved at the Magnum probably assuming I was Prince. I kept it moving though. I finally found who I was looking for on the corner of Brice Street.

Sitting on the stoop in deep conversation with one of his goons, sat Jerome Bennett; A.K.A J-Hood. I hit the horn and beckoned him over. He took his sweet time as he made his approach.

"Damn, what a bitch got to do to get your sexy ass," I asked full of attitude. "You don't call your girl anymore or nothing."

"There you go. Why it always got to be me calling you," he asked as his eyes scanned the block for trouble.

I licked my lips seductively. Hood was my high school sweetheart. Every now and then, we still get together and make sparks fly though. The nigga loved the streets more than moi, so I had to distance myself from his ass. I'm way too spoiled to be competing with the damn block. Had I known then what I know now though, I probably would have stayed.

The block paid off big time for his ass in the long run. Yo paper was as long as Pennsylvania Ave. He got a bitch too that he don't mind spending that paper on also. The nigga kept that hoe dipped in the finest. You might see the bitch pull up to the club sitting pretty in an Audi R8. Rumor is he sends that broad on exclusive shopping sprees all up and down the east coast. Still, the nigga had a weakness for me and it was time to extort those pockets. A bitch was doing bad.

"Jump in real quick. I want to holler at my friend," I said while reaching to pull his belt buckle.

He stepped back out of my reach and put his hands in the air as if surrendering. He pointed at the car.

"Don't think I want to be riding in that car though." He nodded up the street towards his Range. "Let's take my ride."

I started to get a little angry and decided to play with his ego. I commented that his girl had him too shook these days. He waved me off arrogantly.

"Shawty know who the boss is. I want to ride in my car because that shit might be hotter than mine," he said while pointing at the Magnum again. "The streets are talking already. I heard P and Rah got popped yesterday with all that shit."

Fresh

My mouth flew open. This was the first I had heard of this. I should've known something was wrong since Twin, as me and Prince affectionately called each other, didn't call for his car yesterday. I immediately reached for my phone.

"Ma, what's this I'm hearing about Twin and Rah getting locked up?"

I had the phone on speaker. Hood heard my mom as she confirmed the bad news. She told me that Twin was out already though and safely in D.C. with his family. She said that Rah would probably out tomorrow. I felt a lot better after that.

Hood climbed in the passenger seat after I hung up. He reached over and caressed my thigh. I knew where his mind was at. Thinking of the money that he was sure to lay on me made me pull off.

"You got something good to smoke? Hearing that info just fucked my mood up," I confided.

He nodded and directed me to stop at a bodega. Before he got out, I told him to bring me a cranberry juice and two boxes of condoms. He gave me a curious look. I grinned.

"I told you I've been missing you boo," I said sweetly.

* * * * *

(Rah)

I woke up groggy as hell. This county jail isn't for a nigga like me. There was no way I could get used to this shit. First off, they had way too many crackers up in this bitch. Then, they had a nerve to cram all of into an open gymnasium. The beds resembled row boats. We were packed in like sardines too. Out of maybe a hundred inmates, only ten of us were black. White boys were running shit and letting it be known. The TV never turned from MTV. They had smoke and the whole nine. I had to figure out a way to get the fuck out.

Ignoring my aunt's orders, I went straight for the phone and found out that my house number was blocked. I made a mental note right then to change all that once I got out. I tried Princess' number next. Her shit went through, but she didn't answer. I smiled thinking that she would be my three way when she finally woke up later. Big Ma's line went through also but I hung up as soon as it rung. I didn't want to talk to her from nobody's jail. Granny raised me single handedly while the streets possessed my mother. Knowing that I was in jail would probably give her the hives. I dialed my aunt Glo and finally she accepted.

"I know you said not to play these phones aunt Glo, but I called to see what's up with me getting out."

She told me that she understood and gave me the best news that I had ever heard. According to her, I would be out this morning. She explained that she would have gotten me yesterday, but she had to wait on the paperwork for her house to clear.

"I'm glad you called though because you're gonna need a ride from up there. Neither of the twins is answering their phones, and I have court this morning," she stated.

I felt like the weight of the world was let off my shoulders. I quickly gave her the number to my girl and thanked her with all my heart. After hanging up, I started to put a plan together in my head.

First thing I had to do was go see T.O. A lawyer had come yesterday and delivered a message. Now that aunt Glo was getting me out, I wouldn't have to owe him so much. My next move would be to put Prince back on his job with the amigo. With a little luck, I could make a move and solve a lot of my problems.

Chapter 3

(Prince)

I found myself on the highway with only my daughter Asia, in route to visit my pops at the FCI in Petersburg, Virginia. The plan was for the whole family to attend this visit, but for some reason, no one was picking up their phone this morning.

It didn't surprise me that Twin didn't answer. The boy Jay-Z was hosting a party at Love nightclub last night and I'm sure that my sister was in attendance. It did bother me that my mother wasn't in the passenger seat though. After all, this whole visit was her idea. Her reason was probably none other than Darius, her supposed to be fiancé.

Now this dude Darius, I'm not feeling at all. Something just don't sit right with yo, if you ask me. Yo was just too pretty for me. Growing up that pretty in my hood could only mean two things; either you're gay, or you're a playboy. With that said, I just don't like yo. He's the deacon at my mother's church, plus he has plenty of paper. Last I heard fornicating outside of a healthy marriage was a sin. In that case, yo was a hypocrite. He and my mother had been going strong for as long as I can remember. Now they were supposedly engaged. Yo could fool Gloria, but he couldn't fool me.

When we finally reached the prison, it took a whole hour for the racist officers to bring my pops into the visiting room. Bryce Williams strolled into the room with the confidence of a man sure of himself. From the smile on his face, no one in the room could probably tell that he was never getting out.

King, as he is known in the streets, was once the Frank Lucas of Baltimore; minus the snitch factor. Back in the early eighties, a nickel bag wasn't sold in Douglas Projects unless my pops was in on it. A pill of dope couldn't be sold in Park Heights unless it was wearing his "Throne" stamp. A cracker couldn't get a gram of coke out Cherry Hill unless he was buying King's product.

Yo scooped my mom fresh out of high school and wifed her. Not a legal marriage, but a common law one. Pops had everything back then; money, power, and respect. His car game boasted Ferraris, Cadillacs, and Benz's. Yo owned an apartment in the city and a house out in the country. Females practically threw themselves at him, but to my mother's knowledge, he was faithful to her. It's for that reason alone why my mother is still fucking with him twenty years later. When the Feds finally scooped the old man, she was pregnant with me and Twin. She named us Prince and Princess in honor of her King. I stood to give him a hug when he approached.

"Damn...would you look at my grandchild? She's beautiful," he commented while watching Asia play with a little white girl in the nursery. "I sent her a card and a couple of dollars last month for her birthday. Did her mother tell you?"

I nodded my head. My girl Pia told me that she had received a card from him containing four one hundred dollar bills. It amazed her, how he could be at a cashless prison, and still have cash money. It didn't surprise me though. The old man is a natural boss. It was no doubt in my mind that he was still getting his feet wet.

"How's school?"

I told him that all was good with my studies. I explained that I had to bypass summer school this year because I wanted to spend more time with Asia. I wasn't making home too often lately, but all that was about to change. He asked about my mom and Princess. I told him all was good with them and lied that I wanted some one on one time with him. He got straight down to business.

"Heard you want to be a dope boy now? What's up with that," he asked with a little punch to my arm.

I gave him the run down on that situation and how it all occurred. I assured him that the case was clearly an illegal search and seizure. I explained that mom was confident that she would beat it and I told him that Rah was my ace in the hole. Between me and Rah, he had assured me that if push came to shove, he would admit to the drugs before he let me be punished for it. My pops gave me a surprised look.

"That sounds like a winner. Do you really think your cousin would actually do that for you," he asked.

I gave him his same surprised look before assuring him that Rah would definitely hold his own. I told him that there weren't any snitches in the Phillips or Williams' family. He nodded his head, and put his hands up to surrender.

"Slow down playboy! I didn't mean any harm. I was just saying…" He let his words trail off as his eyes scanned the room. "It might not be any rats in the family, but jealousy runs deep. Besides that, I've seen a couple of these dudes paperwork. These Feds will make you tell on your own mother."

The part about ratting on your own mother was stated to make me aware of how jealousy ran in our family. My mother and her twin sister, Toria, are still enemies to this day over jealousy. My aunt Toria is Rah's mother. She was jealous of my mother because she had a crush on my pops first, but he was interested in my mom already. It was a real touchy subject in our family. I still don't have all the details myself.

"Well, I don't have to worry about that type of shit with Rah. We're like this pops...I mean, I trust yo with my life," I emphasized.

Pops nodded his head and leaned forward. He asked why I involved myself in the whole ordeal anyway. He said that the least I could've done was gotten paid for my work. He explained that all I got out of the situation was a case that could possibly land me in a cell beside him.

I thought about what he was saying and had to agree. He was expecting an answer so I gave him the first one that came to mind.

"It's a drought pops. Opportunity was in my face. I don't know, I guess hustling shit is just in me."

"It's in your blood, huh?" He laughed. "Tell me this. Have you ever sold drugs son?"

"I've dabbled," I answered with a nod. "Come on, man. Ma may have that big ass house in Columbia, but you know I'm Westside born and raised. Big Ma still live in the hood, I remind you."

He nodded his head. I started to change the subject, but something wouldn't let me. After a minute of watching Asia play, he turned back to me.

"You said that it's really dry out there, right?" I nodded in agreement. "Let's say for instance I could get maybe fifty kilos of some good shit to you. I'm talking some dope that can be stepped on at least ten times and still be fire. Could you move that much shit and if so, how long would it take you?"

I thought of the question real good before I answered that I could surely move it. I couldn't put a time limit on it because I hadn't ever touched that amount. I did remind him that it was a drought though, and shit was sure to move quickly. He studied me before nodding. His next question was how I would go about moving the work.

"Oh, I'm a smart dude. I definitely wouldn't touch the shit myself. Work of this magnitude, I'll definitely bring Rah in to help me. I know he can certainly make it happen." I snapped my fingers for added emphasis.

Asia finally made her way over to hug her grandfather's neck. He spent the next hour with her. When she disappeared to play again, he started right back where we left off. When the officer finally yelled that visitation was over, he gave me a long hug.

"Remember this number; (410) 737-2891. The password is fifty orders of shrimp fried rice. Follow their directions to the letter. Whatever you do, don't speak to anyone about our conversation today. Don't even tell Rah. The price is fifty stacks a demo. That's two point five million you owe. They'll tell you where to drop the money when you're done. Come back to see me in like two weeks. Remember to keep your cards close to your chest. Use your head and you'll be a millionaire before the year is out."

* * * * *

(Rah)

I had Diamond's face in the pillow and her ass tooted up as I drilled the pussy like a drill sergeant. The X-pill that I had dropped earlier had me like He-Man. I was showing no mercy. She was loving the shit, too.

"Who pussy is this? Huh? Who? Pussy…is….it," I chanted as I thrust into her.

"It's yours Rah! Oh, God, it's yours and you know it," she moaned while tossing her ass back.

I spit on my finger and started to play with her asshole. She immediately reached between her legs and grabbed my nuts to give them a squeeze. This shit drove me crazy and she knew it. Using her pussy muscles, she started to squeeze and milk me like a cow. I fell out the pussy, spent and lay on my back. I dosed off as she used a warm towel to clean me up.

I woke up after midnight. Shorty was nowhere to be found. I dialed her number and got no answer. I tried her sister number and was told that she wasn't there either. It was too late to call her mother's house so I didn't. Fuck it! She was probably out with her girlfriend Tina.

After a long shower, I went naked into the kitchen to get some water. Hadn't shit been going on with me since, I got out of jail. Wasn't much a nigga could do being so broke. I felt like I was in hibernation.

The nigga T.O. wasn't mad at all about his bread. He claimed to be just glad that I was out. I noticed that he didn't tell me to squash the bill, though. I wasn't expecting a miracle like that either.

He did shoot me like ten grand though and instructed me to lay low for a while. That little bread didn't last but a couple of days. I went by his strip club, "Teasers," the other night with a plan. I'm so desperate I broke down and asked for some coke. Fuck it! A nigga got bills and they're not gonna pay themselves. Diamond liked nice things. I got a few shorties on the side that I do for. The rent at my little bachelor pad out in Essex County was due. Basically, it was time to turn my dope shop into a crack spot. Would you believe the nigga had the nerve to laugh in my face and say that he didn't know what I was talking about?

I knew right then that our friendship was over. Yo thought I was hot. His response was a straight sign of disrespect. I'm no punk so I checked him on that shit right then and there. He tried to assure me that he wasn't on it like that, but thought it best I chill for a minute. He wasn't fooling me though.

I knew what I had to do after that night. Drastic times call for drastic measures. I hollered at Prince to contact his amigos first. They said that they would probably know something by the end of the week. After what happened with T.O., I knew I couldn't go to him for a loan. Other niggas probably thought I was hot too. I made my decision then.

The M3 and the Escalade was gonna have to go on the market. Fuck it! They're material things and can be replaced easily anyway. The only backlash I could get from selling my shit was from probably Diamond; but she would just have to get over it. If I could get at least brick money for my two cars, that would be lovely. Fuck asking for permission to move the shit out of the shops and all. Those shits were mine anyway. It was my blood, sweat, and tears that built them. With that in mind, I picked up my phone and called my bitch again.

* * * * *

(T.O.)

I was at my strip club. Beyonce's "Get My Body" blasted from the club speakers. I was sitting on the couch in my back office with five grand in one dollar bills in my hand. Diamond was on the table in front of me with a drink in hand. She was fully clothed, but still doing her thing. Her girlfriend

Fresh

Tina was across the room hugged up with Bruh. Beside me, Diamond's purse laid open. I could see her cell phone lighting up inside. When she turned around to give me a view of that perfect apple shaped ass in those Seven jeans, I snuck a look at who was calling her. Her screen read "Hubby."

I hadn't fucked her yet, but hadn't tried either. I could tell from the flirting that had been going on between us that Rah has a hold on it. It was nothing that I couldn't break. I just wasn't applying the needed pressure yet.

Since we met last week to discuss Rah, conversations over the phone were all that took place. I knew shit was hard on the money tip, so I had tossed her a couple of grand to put in her purse. Basically, I was pumping her for all the info she would provide on her man. Was the nigga acting strange, or what?

My conclusion was simple. I had to cut old boy off. The nigga got caught with too much. If the kilo of dope wasn't enough to alert the Feds, then the money that they found would surely do the trick. I just couldn't take the chance of getting involved in all the nonsense. Back in the day, it was a time I would of put my pit on his ass and been done with it. I couldn't do shorty like that. For some reason, I had a soft spot for him. Right now, my plan was to be patient; keep his shorty close and just write the bread that he owed off like a tax break. Diamond bouncing on the table took me out of my thoughts.

"Do the Oooh...Oooh...Oo...Oo...Oo. Oh. Oh...Ho," she said as she imitated Beyonce's booty hop. Shorty was shaped better than Beyonce in my opinion and could probably give her a run for her money on her own dance. I took a stack of money and tossed it at her feet to encourage her. Her purse was still vibrating like crazy. I decided to tell her because I didn't want old boy getting suspicious. I reached out and pulled her down beside me.

"Your phone is ringing in your purse. It could be your boyfriend," I announced as I nudged her in that direction.

She grabbed her phone, checked the caller ID and cursed out loud. After dialing the number back, she started to yell over the music. Bruh gave me a look and I winked back. After a minute, she hung up and gave me a sad look. I knew what that was about.

"I'm sorry T, but I got to get home. Rah is tripping," she said.

I told her that I understood. There was no need for me to play the jealous role. She started to get herself together. I suddenly had a bright idea.

"Listen, I was thinking that maybe we could fly to Vegas this weekend and do some gambling." Before she could jump to conclusions, I tossed up my hands. "No pressure! I'll even get separate rooms."

She pretended to think for a minute and finally admitted that my plan sounded fun; said that she could maybe figure something out to tell Rah. I told her to get back at me as I helped her gather her money. When she was all set and ready to go, I handed her all of the money. She gave me a crazy look.

* * * * *

(Prince)

I contemplated my father's proposal all week before deciding to move forward. I knew shit wasn't a game. True, I had sold dope before, but never nothing of this magnitude. It was the 2.5 mill that I would owe that had me hesitant. That was a lot of bread.

Could Rah handle that type of money? Should I just dump the whole burden into his lap? Whatever the case, I was real good at math and knew that if shit went right, I was due to make a lot of money. It was that thought and Rah's pressure concerning the amigos, that made me decide to call the number.

As soon as Pia came in from work and relieved me of my babysitting duties, I jumped in my Magnum and headed for B-More. I pulled over at the first payphone I saw and dialed the number. Someone picked up on the first ring.

"Woo's Chinese...How may I take your order?"

"Yes...ah... I would like to order 50 orders of shrimp fried rice," I said nervously into the receiver.

I immediately heard a click and then the dial tone. I stared at the phone in my hand wondering what went wrong. Right when I was ready to try the number again, it rang in my hand.

"Come downtown to Woo's Chinese. We're on 1737 Charles Street. Pull your car around back and honk twice. Someone will tap on your trunk signaling you to open it. Pull off after you hear the trunk close. Call this number back when you're ready to make the money drop."

I heard the dial tone again, said fuck it, and decided to follow orders like pop had told me. The drop went smoothly. As soon as I was out the parking lot, I headed to Federal Hill.

I used my key to open the door to the residence that I was at. The one person I knew I could trust with my secret was sprawled on the couch watching TV. After a quick walk through of the apartment to make sure we were alone, I sat down across from her. My sister gave me a skeptical look.

Fresh

"You want to make fifty thousand dollars, Twin," I asked.

She must've known I was serious by the tone of my voice, because she instantly sat up and started to put on her shoes. I produced a grocery list of all the needed materials that were necessary to get started. Without hesitation, she held out her hand.

"I'm gonna need money to get the shit," she told me.

Chapter 4

(Rah)

Just when I was about to throw in the towel, call up my little goons and go on a robbing spree, a blessing fell into my lap. While sitting around the house playing NBA 2K on my PlayStation 3, a knock suddenly came to my door. After checking the peep hole, I discovered Prince.

"What it look like Cuzzo," I asked as I let him in. "Tell me you got some good news for me."

He ignored the comment and scanned the room. After a moment, he took a seat, produced cigar and asked where Diamond was at.

"She went with her sister to go shop for bathing suits. Her whole family supposed to be going to Ocean City for the weekend," I said as I handed him a trash can to dump his cigar in. "I'm not complaining. Shit, I'm glad she is going. The beach don't cost me shit."

"I know that's right." Prince laughed while concentrating. "I just came back from Philly."

I paused the game, and set up in my seat. The question was in my eyes. For an answer, he reached into his dip and produced what looked like a kilo. I immediately grabbed it and headed for the kitchen. He followed.

"I met Luis' brother while I was down there. It's official cuzzo. We got ourselves a plug. The nigga claims to have unlimited access to the shit."

He pointed to the product. I was busy busting it open. The dope looked nothing like the tar that we had bought a few weeks ago. In fact, I could tell that it was a different kind of dope.

"This shit stink, cuzzo," I said as I put it on my kitchen counter. "Stinking dope means raw dope; and whoever hit this shit did a poor job. If you look close enough, you can actually see the cut sitting on the top of the dope."

"The shit is good though. I stopped through the hood and let Sheila get a test. She knew it was raw from just looking at it cook on her spoon. When I left her, she was in a deep nod."

He tried to pass me the blunt, but I declined. I headed straight for the cabinet to get my gloves, mask, and pills out; ready to work. My adrenaline was at an all-time high. I had my sifting bowl and all laid out before I realized that I didn't have any milk sugar on deck.

"We got to go to the hood. I keep the cut at the spot," I announced before trying to step off.

"Slow down and listen will you." He laughed as he put a hand on my shoulder. "We're stepping our game up with this shit. No more standing in the shop for you. You got to leave that for the workers."

I gave him a look. Cuzzo didn't know what he had here. One brick wasn't enough to keep me out of my shop. As dry as it is these days, this one demo would probably be gone before the morning. He grinned at me and nodded his head.

"I told you the nigga plugged me dog. I got twenty of these shits put up. The tag is seventy five a joint. The faster we move these, the faster and more he'll hit me with." He tried to hand me the blunt again. "Yo didn't give me a time limit for his money, but I really want to make an impression. So I'm thinking you just leave everything as is and put it out there in weight. We put a hundred stack tag on each joint and we each eat nice."

I did the math in my head. If we did shit his way, we were due to profit a quick half a mill. That was like two fifty a piece to split. And as dry as shit is, I can probably be finished in a day or two. Two hundred and fifty grand was good for two days of work.

"And this is how you fuck the game up Rah," he continued. "Let the streets cut their shit down to nothing. You put your boys out there with the shit just like this. I promise you that no one will eat but your boys."

I had to grin at that. Cuzzo was on to something. He was right about the streets cutting their shit real bad to stretch the product. It was only right. Niggas didn't know how long this shit would last. If I put the dope in my shops raw, my boys would get off. I reached out and pulled my cousin into a hug.

"You my nigga…you my nigga…you're my motherfucking nigga," I yelled. "I got you too B. I'm gonna move this shit with no problem. Watch!"

I reached for my phone, but he stopped me. He pointed to the phone in my hand and shook his head.

"You got to dead that phone," he told me. I gave him a dumb look. "Those people had that phone for like three days when you got popped. It isn't no telling what they did to that shit."

I had to nod at his assumption. He tossed me a Motorola pre-paid. I mumbled something about him having shit all figured out while I searched my old phone for my main lieutenant's number. I could trust him to get the shop up and running while I tried to sort this out.

"Yo, who the fuck is this calling my phone from private," my man answered.

"It's me, you Beetlejuice looking motherfucker," I said jokingly. "What the fuck is you up to?"

"Not shit. I'm about to strangle this bitch of mines if she ask me for one more dollar that she know I don't have."

I could feel him loud and clear. Luckily, I had a solution that could change all that. He was ecstatic when I told him this and wanted me to repeat it.

"Just call the troops and have everybody meet you at the trap in an hour. In the meantime, get in your car and come over to my house. I got something for you."

He told me that he was on his job. I hung up and headed for my room. Prince's good news had me all invigorated and shit. I wanted to put on some clothes for a change. When I came out, Prince was enjoying my game of 2K. I asked him was he joining the meeting or what. He stood up and stretched.

"I think I'll pass. I don't want any parts of the labor and if you're smart, you'll lay back as well." He pointed at me. "We're in enough trouble as is. I've found a way to put us both on easy street. It's time you stayed out of the limelight anyway. And whatever you do, don't trust anyone with the info that I gave you this shit."

* * * * *

(Princess)

While Prince was with Rah handling their business, I was in Jessup checking out a little studio apartment to rent for the purpose of keeping the product. The jump-off that I was checking was perfect too. The apartment was located in the downtown area, on top of an old, Afro-Centric miscellaneous store. The owner of the building was a black, divorced and childless woman in her fifties. She didn't look like the snooping type either.

"So what do you think," she asked as we came to the end of our little tour.

"I love it. It's just right for little ole me. The perfect home away from home," I uttered with a smile.

She raised her brow at my choice of words like I knew she would. I already had an excuse ready for her. I told her that I actually was living in D.C. at the moment with my fiancé, but I had just received a summer school teaching internship here in Jessup that I couldn't turn down.

"So you see I'll be in and out a lot. I'll just need this apartment for those nights I'm too tired to make the drive to D.C. Gas is so high these days, you know," I added.

She quickly agreed and looked quite pleased that I was a teacher. She asked what school I would teach at and I gave her what she wanted to hear. As fast as I talked her, I pulled out my wallet and produced my old fake ID that I had since a teenager and a lot of cash.

"Will I need to fill out an application?"

"Oh no honey, that won't be necessary. I own the building. We won't go through all of that.

I'll just write out a formal agreement that you'll have to sign stating that you agree to the conditions. Of course, I'll need an $800 deposit and another $800 for the first month's rent. Water, lights, and cable are all free," she stated while her eyes stayed fixed on the money.

Twenty minutes later I was hauling the duffle bag with the product up the stairs. After locking up, I headed straight to Lowe's to get some new locks for Prince to install.

Back in my Lexus, I thought of the proposition that he had given me. He was paying fifty thousand dollars to play errand girl. My job description was to deliver as many bricks as needed to undisclosed locations that changed daily. For example, when Rah needed product, my duty was to deliver to a church parking lot trash can. Tomorrow, I might deliver to a Walmart dumpster. Even though Rah was the pickup man, he still wouldn't know that it was me delivering the shit. Prince had his shit in order and made sure that I would be protected in my role.

* * * * *

(Gloria)

Tolson, Brooks & Phillips Law Offices occupied the 23rd and 24th floor of the tallest high rise in the city of Baltimore. Located on Lombard Street, from my corner office on the 24th floor, I had a perfect view of the harbor and the many boats docked there. My office was spacious and expensively decorated. I sat at my desk and studied the police report of my son's case that had been delivered earlier today.

The police basically wrote the incident up the way that Prince explained it. They really had no reason to pull them over to begin with. The offices lied and said some shit about the passenger acting strangely while parked at the service station and through his police training he deduced that Prince was nervous during questioning at the initial stop.

They also said the dog alerted to drugs in the car which prompted the search. I wasn't worried about the dogs. It was a proven fact that those fucking dogs alerted to almost 75% false alarms. The drugs were found in a secret compartment. After a series of tests and experiments on the vehicle, there was no sequence of maneuvers or combinations to get into the compartment. No finger prints were found on the money, drugs or anywhere near the compartment. Basically, they had zip and were crazy if they thought my boys were going down for those drugs. I quickly buzzed my secretary.

"Laura, get me Johnny Thornton out of the investigative department. Ask him to stop by my office immediately when he is available. I also need you to make an appointment with Randy Traynor for me. Tell him it's about the discovery of my nephew's case. The preliminary is set for next week and I think we should be on the same page."

The firm employed in-house private investigators. Thanks to me, Johnny headed the department. Our relationship went back to the days when I was doing my own thing. When I came to this firm, I brought him along. As I moved up the ladder, so did he. For my services, his loyalty to me was above all else. He was in my office only fifteen minutes after my request. I slid the discovery to him once he sat down. He scanned it with a raised brow.

"This Prince Williams; is he your boy," he questioned.

"The one and only," I replied. "I need you to copy that discovery and check it out for me from a cop's point of view. Go up to Cecil County and dig up all the dirt you can. I need crooked cops, sour D.A.'s and poisoned judges. See if that store in question has surveillance footage of that day."

Johnny nodded his head. He understood me loud and clear. He knew my motto and that I am a born winner. I rarely lose a case, hate to plea bargain and by no means represent rats. If a witness can be bought, I'll pay. If a little perjury is needed, I'll lie. By any means necessary is what I try to live by.

* * * * *

(T.O.)

Fresh

I was just climbing into the back of my Maybach when I saw an unmarked Crown Victoria pull onto my lot. I cringed when I saw the driver climb out and come my way.

"Mind if I join you in the backseat of this mini apartment," he joked while not waiting to be invited in. "Always wanted to see what all the hype was about with these things. How does she drive?"

"I wouldn't know Barry," I responded seriously. "I just know how the backseat rides."

Chief Barry Stevens of the Baltimore Police Department could only shake his head. Our relationship started in high school. He was actually raised on my block. We had been friends for the longest time. Something told me that this wasn't a friendly visit, however. I was late for a visit with my lawyer to discuss my divorce proceedings. After a glance at my watch, I asked him what I could do for him.

"It's been a lot of traffic over on Brice lately. You boys back in business," he asked.

Brice was a block that Rah controlled personally. However, there were a few crack houses on that strip also. I was about to mention that before he added that traffic had also doubled on Augusta & Fredericks, Montford & Oliver, Biddle & Castle and a couple other known dope spots in the city.

It was evident that it was some dope in B-more and he wanted his cut. I told him that I was still out of commission and reminded him that I didn't own the city.

"However, I'll put my ear to the streets and find out what's up. If it's any of my boys pumping, I'll make sure you get your cut."

He got the message and quickly exited the vehicle. Fucking with me, he made the easiest money of his life. Every month I paid him one hundred grand to keep the heat off my traps. Since my dope shops had been shut down, he still pulled in half of that ransom for my coke spots. Obviously, his co-conspirators' palms were getting dry. As soon as he was out the car, I directed Bruh to the Westside of town. While on the way, I called my lawyer.

"Something's come up Randy. You can handle the deposition until I get there right? I'm not really tripping, though. Agree to anything she wants as long as it's reasonable," I ordered.

We made it to the hood pretty fast. I could tell shit was up and running from first glance. Fiends were lined up all over the place, while the dope boys gave instructions. Personally, it had been a while since I had witnessed shit so alive around these parts.

Bruh circled the west without a word. I witnessed a couple of Rah's boys calling shots and reached for Bruh's phone. Rah's phone went straight to voicemail. I could've called his girl to milk her for info, but chose to see what was popping around the hoods first.

After circling the city, I concluded that there was dope around. I had Bruh drop me at the lawyer's office and told him to find out what he could. When he picked me up, he had some news.

"Spoke to Styles over East Baltimore. He said the man with the plan is you boy Rah. Said he thought the shit he bought was coming from us," Bruh reported.

Rah had definitely made a power move. The nigga Styles had shops that rivaled mine. He was good for at least ten demos a week and usually copped heavy. My thoughts right now were where was rah getting the product to sell weight. I asked Bruh did Styles say how much he copped.

"I didn't get all in the boy's business like that. He did mention that the work was fire though. He said something about it being the best we've had in a while."

I dialed Rah's number again and got the same results. With no other resolution, I dialed his girl's number.

"What's up gorgeous? Are we gambling this weekend, or what?"

"Damn...I was just about to call you," she stated cheerfully. "Everything is a go this way. I told old boy that I was going up to Ocean City with my family."

I told her that I would call the travel agency and get our flight info. In the meantime, I asked was she sure Rah believed her story.

"Believe me, trust is not an option in this house; especially, when it comes to me. On another note, my family is really going to the beach, so all is good."

I peeped that she had said "in this house." That let me know that she was in fact home right then and Rah obviously wasn't there. I casually asked where he was.

"I don't even know. I been running in and out all day and he hasn't been here. I think I'll call him after we hang up and be nosy."

I decided to let her get on top of that then.

* * * * *

(Rah)

The same way that Prince had showed up at my door unexpectedly earlier, I was showing up at his now. It was a quarter 'til nine and I was already done with the work. His girl Pia, a half Korean, half Black beauty, answered the door.

"Oh, hey Rah," she answered while giving me a quick hug. "Your cousin is upstairs giving Asia a bath. I'll go get him."

Fresh

The smell of cube steak got my attention and I headed to the kitchen. A nigga had been on the move so much today that I hadn't even stopped to eat. I yelled upstairs and asked Pia could I grab a bite.

"Help yourself. We've already eaten, but be sure to wash your hands," she yelled down.

By the time Prince finally made it downstairs, I was washing my plate off. He grabbed a cigar I had put on the table and started to twist up.

"It's a wrap Cuz," I said over my shoulder.

"What's a wrap?"

"The work," I answered nonchalantly while picking rice from between my teeth. "I got the bread in my whip. Didn't feel like lugging that big bag up in here."

Prince looked at me as if I was joking. The question was in the air; twenty kilos in one day. That's one point five million for the plug and another four hundred thousand to split between the two of us. Plus I was still due some cash from my shops. My nigga Murder had checked in and reported that shit was moving along swiftly at the traps. In all, I would be bringing in an easy two mill for ten hours of work.

"Ain't no money like dope nigga," I said with a wink.

"You can say that again," he added while shaking his head. "I can't believe shit moving like that."

I snapped my fingers and gave him a rundown of the day's activities. After straightening my shops out, I contacted Styles from over East and the boy Swift from Cherry Hill. They took all that shit off my hands and even put in orders for more.

"That's crazy yo. A little dope hit the streets and all types of money come out the wood works. And they got the nerve to say it's a recession. Now you know who got all the fucking money," Prince said with a yawn.

"I know right. But check, go ahead and call your boy. I need to know what's up so I can tell these worrisome ass niggas something," I stated as I made my way towards his front door. A nigga felt drained for some reason.

"Fuck them niggas, Cuzzo! I already told you that we wasn't rushing no more. We gonna move on our time," he announced while handing me the blunt to light.

I nodded my head. It was his show and I was content on letting him run it the way he saw fit. I still asked him what I was supposed to be doing while he made moves. His answer was for me to just be patient. When we made it to my whip, I popped the trunk and pointed to a Gucci carryall.

Fresh

"That's the plug's money and yours. I counted the shit and separated it," I said as I gave him dap. "I put my extra money counter in there with it too. You can keep that one but I'm gonna need the Gucci bag back. You know how Diamond is about her shit."

He teased me that I could afford another bag and snatched up the satchel. I got in my whip and told him to be safe on his drive.

Chapter 5

(Princess)

"Isn't that your aunt right there girl," my best friend Shy'Quita asked.

I quickly looked to the left side of the street. There, on a stoop in front of an abandoned row house, was my aunt busy waving me down. I pulled over to the curb and waited on her.

My mother's twin sister, Victoria, sprinted towards my car like she was in a track meet. I hadn't seen her in months and was anxious to check for her. Even though the streets possessed her, she was still my flesh and blood. I got out the car as she approached to hug her neck, but she took a step back and pointed at her shirt.

"Watch yourself. I had an accident earlier with some of this fuck shit these boys are out here selling." She pointed at a stain that looked like dried throw up on her shirt.

Like my mother, aunt Toria had a mouth on her. Once a beauty herself, it hurt my heart to see how the streets were slowly eating away at her. She looked like a dead woman walking.

Fresh

"Where the hell you been auntie? I was with Big Ma a couple of weeks ago and she told me that you hadn't been by to see her in a while," I said.

"Girlllll…I been busy. I live out the county now with my boyfriend. I got his damn mouth tore off. Yo won't let me out of his sight. I had to literally break up with his ass to get away this time."

I leaned back against my whip trying to decipher whether she was lying or not. Knowing her, she probably was. I asked her where she would be staying now that she was back.

"Probably with Ma; I been so busy partying that I haven't gotten around there yet. You know I can't stand for Ma to see me like this," she said pointing at her shirt again. "But enough about me, look at you girl; looking like you stepped out of a Vogue magazine ad. Where are y'all headed to?"

I looked down at the Fendi blouse, skirt and matching boots that I had on. I was only heading to the hair salon, but was dressed as if I was going to the club. Getting fly every day is just my M.O. and she should've known that.

"Oh, I'm just heading up Pennsylvania Avenue to my girl's shop," I relayed while digging in my purse to give her a couple of dollars. "Put this in your pocket in case you get hungry. Oh, and I went through my closet the other day. I got a lot of cute summer shit for you."

It was a lie, but I made a mental note to really make that happen. I always blessed her with my last year's wear. She nodded her head vigorously while stuffing the forty bucks I had handed her. After asking about Prince and Rah, we parted ways.

Back in my whip, Quita was busy putting the finishing touch on a blunt she was rolling while yapping to some nigga over her cell. I heard her mention the upcoming Jeezy concert and knew what she was up to. Shorty is a gold digger with a capital G.

Unlike me, she don't have the luxury of having her mother take care of her. In fact, she don't have any family still alive in Baltimore, period. Her mother passed a couple years ago due to an overdose. Luckily, she was nearly eighteen and was ready to take care of herself.

Anyway, shorty was a fly chick in her own right. She was just hood as hell. Niggas didn't like that fly mouth of hers unless it was in their lap. She had no problems obliging either as long as a nigga had the dollars to pay. Like me, she liked the finer things in life. Whatever the case, after the confirmation of a new outfit from whoever she was on the phone with, she hung up and sparked the blunt. I asked her who was donating.

"That tight ass nigga I told you about who took me to New York with him," she said with a wave of the hand. "I'm not even studying his ass though. I'm thinking about those Jimmy Choos' I seen on Fifth Ave and 51st. Girl, them bitches were so tight. They was only like six something too; and can you believe old boy didn't want to kick. That's alright though 'cause you know he gots no play for that stunt. I thought that was the end of his ass but I guess he back sniffing around."

I laughed out loud, but my mind was really on the fifty grand I was due tomorrow. Prince had me drop another load off to Rah this morning. It was nothing but thirty of them things left altogether. At the rate Rah was moving them, I didn't expect for them to last long.

"But fuck that clown; I'm checking for my future husband," Quita continued. "Where the fuck is he at?"

I told her that he was probably in D.C. with his kid's mother. Just as I suspected, she copped a real attitude at that statement.

"Damn, that Oriental bitch got that nigga fucked up. The nigga been home like three weeks and I haven't seen him not once," she whined.

I just shook my head. She and Prince had history. They were actually a couple back in the days. In fact, Prince was the only nigga I had ever seen control her. They ended their relationship because the streets got in his ear about the few miles Quita had on her. They still got together every now and again though. I asked why she hadn't called him, as we pulled up to the salon.

"I have been calling him, but I think he's screening calls." She gave me a curious look to see if I knew anything.

I knew the real reason she wasn't getting through, but couldn't tell her. Yo wasn't fucking with his old phone after that locked up situation and it wasn't my place to pass out his new number. If he wanted her to have it, he would've gotten in touch with her. I did remind her that he would definitely be at the concert though.

* * * * *

(T.O.)

"So that's what's up. We'll meet at Dulles in the morning at nine sharp in front of the American Airlines terminal," I stated while winking at Bruh.

I was on the phone with Diamond confirming the last minute details of our trip. Shorty was all ready to go.

"Oh God, I can't believe I'm actually doing this. I've never…" She paused for a second. "Hold on, I have to answer this."

I was glad she got the beep. We were too far in the game to be getting cold feet on me now. We have only been talking for two weeks and I'm starting to crave her sexy ass. When she came back on the line, we conversed a few more minutes and then hung up.

I still hadn't spoken with or seen Rah since he had somehow flooded the town. Not wanting to leave the city without bumping into him, I had to stoop low as to call on my good friend down at the station to put out an APB on him. I got the call that his car was spotted at Eldorado's titty bar on Lombard a little while ago. Me and Bruh was just pulling up there now.

I had no problem spotting him when we made it in the joint. He was near the stage along with two other cats tossing dollars to the ladies. We made our way in his direction. His man spotted us first and nudged Rah. To my surprise, Rah didn't flinch when he seen me. Instead, he moved over for us to be seated.

"What's popping, old timer," he asked while getting the bartender's attention. He asked what we were drinking.

Since he was big spending, I told the bartender to bring me a bottle of Louis XIII and motioned for two glasses. I let my eyes scan my surroundings and spotted Rah's cousin Prince sitting to his right. They were hanging tight, which meant that they were probably getting the work from Philly. Once the drinks were poured, Rah slid close.

"What the fuck are you doing downtown; checking out the competition?"

"You could say that," I answered with a nod. "I had to come see what was driving all of my customers, such as yourself, down here. That, and the fact that I wanted to see your face; make sure you're good, you know."

"Me," he asked with a raised eyebrow. "I'm good fam; real good. Just trying to stay low and under the radar."

I told him that low and under the radar was a good thing, but the statement was hard to believe because his name was all that I'm hearing in the streets these days. He gave me a stupid look that sort of pissed me off. I decided to get down to business.

"Cut the bullshit Rah. You know what I'm talking about. Let me find out that you're ducking a nigga?"

He downed his drink in one swallow and shook his head. He told me that he wasn't ducking me and was fully aware of the money that he owed; said that he was making moves to get that to me ASAP.

I didn't want the money that he owed me. In fact, I had already marked that off as sort of a tax write off. I wanted to know what was up with the work and asked him about it.

"Shit short, old timer. I'm at the bottom of the barrel," he said, not missing a beat. "But I can get that money I owe to you as soon as tomorrow."

I decided to tell him that the money wasn't important and he could keep it. I told him that if he wanted to do something for me, then he could get me some of that anthrax that he was around here selling. He nodded and seemed to be in deep thought. After the bartender brought him another drink, he turned on me.

"On the real Unc, I can't call it right now. Everything happened so fast that I don't really know what's going on. But let me holler at yo and see what's good. As soon as I know something, I'll get back to you."

I checked him out to see if he was bullshitting me. The look he gave me was sincere. I gave him a pound, told him that I was heading out of town for the weekend and that he could reach me at the shop first thing Monday.

* * * * *

(Prince)

I made the drive down to Petersburg alone this time. The guards took their sweet time getting me processed in. When my father came out, we got right down to business.

"I'm impressed," were the first words out of his mouth. "My people told me that you handled your business in no time."

I wanted to smile, but decided to keep my poker face. He wanted to know how I pulled it off and I told him everything. I told him how I received the work boxed up in candles. Explained that I only put a three on the product to keep it legit and that it could have easily took another hit or two. After getting the shit bricked up, I passed it off to Rah and he made it happen.

He nodded showing no sign of emotion. When he finally spoke, he inquired about the money I made. I broke it down that we pulled in close to twelve million in all; told him that after Rah collected his two mill, that left us ten to split.

"That's what's up," he said with a nod. We got up to get some drinks. When we got back, he asked what my next move would be. I didn't know if he was springing a trick question on me so I decided to give him what I thought he wanted to hear.

"Shit, I'm ready to move whenever you are. The streets ate that shit up and are hungry for more," I said confidently.

"Son, when I asked what your next move would be, I wasn't asking if you were ready for more product. That shit on deck for you whenever you want it. It's a proven fact that you can make the money. What I was trying to figure out was what do you plan to do with the money?"

He had me baffled with that one and I guess he could see the question in my eyes. Luckily, he saved me the embarrassment of asking.

"We need to find a way to start cleaning up that money now, son. You see, the game has advanced ten-fold since I was last out there. You just made ten million dollars in less than a week. Son, not even I have seen that type of cash that fast. You can't tell these white folks that though, and that's my fault. You see, I made a couple mill look like fifty million when I had it. I spent money so recklessly, that I was practically begging for them to come get me. I had the house, ten cars and all the finer things. The one thing that I didn't have was a means to show that I could afford these nice things. I didn't have a job son; a steady paycheck. Had I shown a means of income, I probably wouldn't be here today," he said while pointing at the table in front of him.

I heard the stories and could feel him. Big Ma and them used to tell me about the extravagant lifestyle that he lived. I had already thought of that. Shit, at the moment, I was still in shock that I had so much money that I hadn't thought about spending a dime of it.

"I feel you Pops. I have no problem working either. The only problem is getting a good enough job to compensate for a nice purchase," I told him.

"I've been thinking of that. I might just have the answer," explained. "I'm thinking that this is where we bring your mother into the picture."

I cut him off right then. It was no way that I was bringing mom into this thing. I didn't even want her to know that I was selling drugs period. Sure, she use to be ride or die all the way, but she had changed over the years and I told him that. He had other plans, though.

"I feel where you are coming from, but really, it's no way around her coming in. Think about it. Your mother brought in one point five million last year. That's legit money. If push ever came to shove and the Feds ever get involved, who better to back us with an income than your mother?"

He had a good point there. Once he seen that I was going for it, he told me to let him handle my mother and for me to handle the streets. I still wasn't convinced but I had no reason not to trust him. We used the rest of the visit to outline my next pick up for the work.

* * * * *

(Raheem)

Fresh

"Yo, I'm about to keep it moving. Y'all niggas be safe out here," I said to my man Gutta as we stood on Pennsylvania Avenue in front of the dope shop he ran.

"Yeah, I feel you. It must be nice to ride around all day while niggas like myself got to get their hands dirty. I feel you big dog," Gutta joked as I walked off.

I could've taken his comment as a low blow of jealousy, but I didn't. There wasn't any animosity in the air these days that I was aware of. In fact, niggas was more on my dick for breathing some fresh life into these streets.

I laughed at his statement and headed to my car. The sun was shining bright today, a nigga's safe is stacked high again and my girl was out of town. I had the rest of the day to kick around and do nothing until the Jeezy concert tonight. There wasn't shit left for me to do, but get some pussy. So I strolled through my phone in search of the number of a broad that I met last night.

"Hello?"

"Is this Kim," I asked.

"Yes, this is she. Who is this?"

"It's your boy Rah. You gave me your number..."

"Oh yeah, hey, I know exactly who this is!"

I smiled at the enthusiasm in her voice. After checking my blind side, I crept out into traffic and went into Mack mode.

"What's up? How you doing," she asked.

"I'm taking it easy. Was thinking about you and decided to check for you."

"That's what's up. I'm not doing too much. Was about to cook myself something," she informed.

"Don't do that," I told her.

"What do you mean, don't do that? A girl got to eat, you know."

"I know that, but I was trying to come get you and take you out for something to eat."

"Is that right?"

I was in rare form and ready to trick. From experience, I knew the quickest way to the panties was to spend a couple of dollars.

"Yeah, I was thinking that we could grab a bite to eat and then head over to this little boutique called Gucci to pick you out a nice outfit for the concert tonight."

"Aren't you the generous one? All this sounds good, but tell me exactly what you'll be expecting in return for your generosity and I'll think about it," she asked sneakily.

"All I want is the pleasure of putting a smile on your face. That and the fact that I get to watch you model your gift for me."

Fresh

I tried to sound as innocent as possible. Maybe I had jumped this one wrong. Any other broad would've leaped at the opportunity for a free meal and some Gucci. Whatever the case, shorty might've been skeptical, but she wasn't crazy. After issuing out an address in north B-more, she told me that I could scoop her in twenty minutes.

It was right after hanging up with her and concentrating on my surroundings that I peeped a suspicious looking black Impala two cars behind me. I instantly pulled over at the next Arab store that I saw. As the Impala passed, I noticed that it was definitely an unmarked. I jumped out my Beemer and proceeded into the store to get some blunts. When I came out, the Impala was nowhere in sight.

"Nigga, you tripping," I said out loud to myself as I got back into my whip. Just to be on the safe side, I decided to roll up and watch the streets at the same time.

No sooner than I pulled back into traffic, a black Crown Vic got in on my tail. I knew I was in trouble once I swung a left on Castle. The Jake followed. Before, the Impala trailed two cars behind me. This Vic was dead in my ass. I took a deep breath and tried to get my thoughts together.

I didn't have any drugs but the blunt I had just rolled. I sat that in the ashtray in front of me and tried to calm my nerves. My next thoughts were exactly which law enforcement agency was behind me. It was just possible that these could be DEA agents inquiring about that highway incident. My mind was so far out there, I hadn't even noticed that the first Impala was now in front of me. A glance to my left produced a whole different Crown Vic. They had boxed me in and were forcing me to pull over. This wasn't your average routine traffic stop. In no time, I found myself surrounded by black and white faces with guns pointed at me.

"Get those hands up! I need to see those hands," I heard a familiar voice yell.

When I saw the officer to my left, I almost wanted to grin. Luckily this wasn't the Feds. Lt. Jack Walsh of the BDP headed the Drug Task Force in the city. I knew him pretty well from the old neighborhood. Yo and his crew are ruthless and as crooked as they come. I knew instantly that this was just a shakedown.

"Whoa yo, be easy with that steel," I urged with my hands in plain view.

They snatched me out the whip, searched me and led me to their patrol car in no time. Walsh told his cronies to search the car, while he spoke with me for a minute. As soon as he got in the car, I let him know that I wasn't happy about his harassment.

"Yo, Walsh, what the fuck, man! Tell your peoples…"

Fresh

He cut me off instantly. Told me to listen to what he had to say and listen well. Once he knew that he had my attention, he started to speak very slowly as if I was a mental patient or something.

"First, I'm gonna tell you what I already know. Then I'm gonna tell you what I can do. And last, I'm gonna propose a solution to the problem."

I heard him and heard him clearly, but my mind was on my whip. It was a known fact that his goons were notoriously jealous of the hustlers' cars and made a point to vandalize shit. I let Walsh know that he had my attention, but instructed him to calm his boys down. He gave me a sarcastic look before answering.

"That car and what my officers find will be the least of your worries if you just follow my lead." He nodded his head, assuming that I got his point. "Now this is what's really good. You know me and know what I do. I can be an enemy or your best friend. With that said, I have been hearing your name a lot in these streets lately. In fact, I have more than one trusted informant telling me that you are the man to see these days."

I started to shake my head; told him that he knew me from way back and assured him that he had his people fucked up. His answer was ruthless.

"Either cut the bullshit Rah or I'll tell Sgt. Lee up there to bring me that half a kilo and pistol that he just found in your trunk back there. That'll look real good to go along with that other case that you just caught on 95 recently," he threatened.

I submitted with my eyes. It was no doubt in my mind that he would make good on his threat to plant that shit in my car. I was in a no win situation and he knew it. He patted me on the arm and went into good cop mode.

"Look, I'm not asking you to admit to anything. I know you're a stand up kid and have a lot of street smarts." He took out a cigarette, offered me one and then lit up. "And like I told you before, I'm trying to make shit look good for everyone. So this is what it is. I know you are the man to see. I know you got them things going for a hundred a pop. I know that in the addition to what you got going on in the old neighborhood, you've just partnered with Gutta and them boys over on Pennsylvania. I know that if all this is true, you're about to be one rich young man," he ended with a laugh.

Yo knew his business. The new shop on Pennsylvania had just opened yesterday. My man Gutta, who ran things over that way, had fallen on bad times due to the drought. He didn't want to lose his shop totally so he approached me with a partnership that I couldn't turn down. In exchange for me supplying the work, he would let me eat. Pennsylvania Ave is a known gold mine. Walsh

Fresh

exhaled smoke into my face to let me know he wasn't finished.

"I guess you can see that I've done my research. So let's get on to what I can do if I choose to. I think that you already know I'm capable of shutting shit down at both of the traps. I can put 24 hour surveillance on you to make your life a living hell. I can also call one of my friends at the DEA and give them everything that I have on you..."

I was through bullshitting myself. Yo had me down bad. I could sit and let him extort me on his terms or I could set some rules of my own.

"How much," I asked simply.

"One hundred grand," he replied. "One hundred a month that is."

I pretended that his price was outrageous, started whistling and shaking my head and screwing up my face. He shook his head; told me that a hundred grand was bird feed to the money I was making. I pretended to ponder his offer before finally asking what a hundred grand would get me.

"Protection for the shops of course; as long as you continue to run shit in an organized fashion, we can make it happen. If you have any trouble that I can help out with, I'll do my part. And of course, if anybody starts asking questions in the department, I'll steer them in another direction."

I still acted like I wasn't convinced. I whined about the tag and brought up the fact that the hood shops were already protected.

"I have mouths to feed," he stated while nodding at his boys. "And as far as the hood being protected, you're wrong. I don't know what's going on in your camp, but I just got word that certain people don't control the dope in this city anymore. Therefore, all dope shops are open season and up for renegotiation."

It wouldn't be the first time I paid the police and probably wouldn't be the last. I agreed to his terms and set a few of my own.

Fresh

Chapter 6

(Gloria)

As headstrong and independent as I claim to be, it's hard to believe that I have any weaknesses. Unfortunately, I do have a few and their names are King, Prince and Princess. As soon as I got word from Prince that his father wanted to see me, I made the necessary arrangements to have a lawyers' visit.

Unlike a regular visit, my process to enter the facility was a lot easier. After signing in, having a quick photo taken and getting my briefcase scanned for contraband, I was escorted into a small room with a see through window for the guard to peep in at us when needed. King was waiting inside, busy looking through a file that was no doubt his latest appeal paperwork.

"Good evening Mr. Williams," I greeted for the guard's amusement as I entered the room.

King smiled and nodded while taking in my appearance. No doubt, I took pride in looking good daily, but of course I had to do a little extra for my Beau. Nothing spectacular, though because I still had to keep everything professional. Today, I chose a thin white Prada business suit, unbuttoned at the shop to show a little cleavage, while the pants hugged my figure to perfection.

"Well good evening to you also," King stated after the guard had took his leave. "And to what honor do I owe this unexpected visit?"

I peeped at the guard to make sure he wasn't in my mouth before whispering that I missed him and decided to get up here ASAP after his son relayed the message.

He seemed to enjoy that response and launched into a conversation about his children. I told him about cutting his daughter's allowance due to excessive spending and informed him that I was somewhat worried lately because she hadn't called asking for anything. Afterwards, I told him about Prince getting indicted for his case, but assured him that I had that situation under control.

He asked about his aunt Ruby, who was his only living relative besides me and the kids. She raised him and he loved her like a mother. Out of love for him, I retired her to an upscale rest home out in Baltimore County. Though I hadn't been to check on her recently, I told him that I would get right on it.

"Is there anything else, Mr. Williams," I asked in my best lawyer voice.

For an answer, he glanced around and then leaned in to steal a kiss. He asked me how I had been and wanted to know if my friend was treating me good. I melted instantly. Though I loved Darius dearly, he couldn't hold a candle to this man in front of me. In a sad way, I hated myself for being so weak for King.

"I've been okay, I guess. Working hard," I replied.

He wouldn't let me ignore his latter question and promptly mentioned Darius again. I started to go in defense mode, but he stopped me.

"Listen, I only asked about you and his situation because I'm aware that y'all are supposed to be getting married soon and I wanted you to hold that off for a little while; at least until after the election this year," he suggested.

I ignored his question again, but asked why he wanted me to wait until after the elections. He glanced around nervously before answering. He lowered his eyes and mumbled something about him maybe getting out before the New Year.

I sat back and crossed my arms at my chest. I couldn't believe that he still had the balls to carry me like some young chick. True, back in the days, I believed all of his get out of jail dreams but this was a new day. In fact, I'm the one who filed his last two appeals. I know everything it is to know about his case; had already argued every loophole available. Wasn't nothing getting this man out of prison but…I stopped in my tracks. If I heard him right, he had just spoken of the election. I gave him a stern look.

"Bryce Orlando Williams," I scolded. "What in the hell are you up to?"

He grinned, scooted a little closer for privacy and asked me what I knew about a dude name Michael Katz; also known as the Jew. I raised an eyebrow. The name was familiar. It all started to come back to me.

"Big time lobbyist; was rumored to be the go to man in Washington for big business. Wasn't too much that he couldn't get done; no strings that he couldn't get pulled. If my memory serves me correct though, isn't he locked up somewhere for tax evasion or something," I asked.

For an answer, King nodded. He told me that Katz was currently locked up with him; said that the guy was so powerful in Washington that he pulled strings to get a lot of the charges dropped and only ended up with sixty months. I nodded as if impressed and asked what all this had to do with him getting out.

"It's simple," he answered nonchalantly. "The guy's son is still out there making moves for him. A lot of people owe this guy favors bae. According to him, he guaranteed me a full pardon out of here for a hefty fee."

In my lifetime, I had seen this man do some pretty amazing things. It wasn't much that surprised me about him. He always promised me that even though he was sentenced to life, that wouldn't deter him from getting out one day. Call me crazy if you want, but I always believed him. If I was hearing him correctly today, then this was his way out. No President in office had ever pardoned a man with a life sentence, yet alone pardoned a man with a record like King's. I somehow believed that this was the big one though.

"You're planning to bribe the President of the United States," I asked just to be sure.

For the answer, he simply nodded his head and smiled. My mind went into instant overdrive. In less than a minute, I had recounted our whole conversation. I added in this Michael Katz history and tallied up that with enough money and a lot of luck, this could possibly go down. After all, our sitting President was almost capable of anything. I asked him just how much this whole thing was going to cost.

"Fifteen million; ten for the White House and five for my friend," he answered.

I almost cursed out loud, but not because the price was so high. For what he was planning to pull, the price was actually reasonable. My aggravation stemmed from how I was supposed to raise the money. My house was worth a little over a million. I have another two million in mutual funds and half that much in municipal bonds. On paper, I'm only worth close to four mill. Sure, I could probably get a substantial loan from the bank, but… Bottom line, King was gonna have to pull a rabbit out of the hat to help me.

"Baby, I have four, maybe five mil that I can donate to the cause," I told him calmly but confidently. "Now I'm with you all the way. I know you have a plan in the works so just run it down to me and see what's what."

He took my hand in his; told me that he knew that he could count on me and that he did already have a plan in the works. I nodded and smiled, happy that his man knew me so well.

"I have already raised five million of the money and the way things are looking, I can put the remaining change together also. What I need from you is to listen to what I have to say and to trust me."

I was already all ears. He had my full and undivided attention. After all, I'm a lawyer. Listening is what I do best. I told him that I was listening and reminded him that I was with him 100%. It was the truth too. For him, I was prepared for anything. Anything except what came out of his mouth next that is.

He started by running down how he had met a Chinese connection here in prison. He said that he had put his connection on the get out of jail plan in exchange for the man getting some dope shipped here to Baltimore. He explained that his operation had only been going on for a few weeks, but due to the drought, he had been able to accumulate all this bread.

My finding out that he was back in the drug game didn't surprise me. After all, he's a hustler by nature. Getting money is in his DNA. What pissed me off was when he told me he had our son running his little dope empire. I immediately went off on his ass.

"Not my son; are you out of your fucking mind," I yelled, but quickly calmed down when I remembered where we were.

He reached out a hand to calm me and begged me with his eyes to calm down; told me to at least hear him out like I'd promised.

I noticed the guard start to get nosy so I smiled. Once he turned back to his magazine, King continued. He explained how he and Prince had set up a system where as Prince only gave the stuff to Rah and evidently, Rah handled all the dirty work.

This still didn't settle my nerves. I've dealt with enough cases to know that the Feds made cousins snitch out cousins. The Federal system was notorious for turning people into snitches. I didn't voice this to him because I was sure he was aware. Instead, I just listened.

"Listen bae, I promise not to have our son in harm's way. In fact, I got just enough dope delivered to gather the funds that we need. After it's gone, I swear to you that I'll pull Prince out. You do believe me don't you," he asked. After studying him for a moment I nodded. "Now you said that you would help so this is what I need you to do…"

* * * * *

(Prince)

I woke up naked and not in my own bed. I could hear my phone vibrating in the distance. After surveying my surroundings, and hearing a certain voice in the kitchen, I concluded that I was at Shy'Quita's house.

I bumped into shorty at the Jeezy concert the other night. As usual, she was looking like a winner and on my dick. I wanted to get at her that night, but couldn't risk it because Pia was in the place along with a couple of her friends. However, that didn't stop me from making future plans, which led me to this morning's events. I came over after dropping Asia off at daycare. When I arrived at her crib, we quickly made up for lost time.

The bedside clock read 2:18. That gave me just enough time to get dressed and make the trip to D.C. to pick up my seed. I yelled for Quita, who was obviously in the kitchen whipping up something to eat. Shorty was butt ass naked when she entered the room and I instantly started to regret that I had to leave.

"Please don't tell me that you're trying to leave so soon," she whined while handing me the phone.

I grabbed the phone and spoke into the receiver, already knowing that it was my sister on the line. Quita dropped straight to her knees and started to release my dick from the confines of my boxers.

"Your mother is calling around looking for you," Princess warned.

"Word?"

"Yep, said something about you getting in touch with her ASAP. She sounded pissed too," Princess exhaled.

Quita had me trapped. She knew her business and knew it well. She had her hands on my chest, fingering my nipples while she bobbed her head in a deep throat fashion. She knew how to please me like no other. The secret to her success was that she actually enjoyed giving head. I reached over and ran my fingers through her pussy lips. As I suspected, shorty was wetter than a motherfucker. I slapped her across the ass. That only made her moan and take more of me into her throat.

"Are you listening to me," Princess yelled and got my attention. "What in the hell...Y'all are some nasty motherfuckers!"

She promptly hung up and I literally threw the phone. Quita brought me to a climax a minute after that. Of course she wanted me to fuck her afterwards, but I begged off explaining that I had to pick up Asia. I decided to call my mother while on the beltway.

"What up Ma," I asked when she answered.

"Nothing much; I'm just coming from visiting your father."

My heart dropped into my stomach. She knew…I hadn't expected her to find out until the weekend. Evidently, she had made a special visit today. I tried to sound nonchalant.

"Word, what was the old man talking about?"

"You know your father, still thinking he's the smartest man on earth. He reminds me of you really. Both of you think that y'all are so slick."

She was trying to disguise how pissed she was, but I knew she was hot. I should've never let my father tell her. I mean, my mother was cool and all, but it's just some shit that she can't understand. My being involved with drugs with so much to lose was definitely one of those things.

"I should be in the city within the next hour. I have to stop by Big Ma's and then I plan to go by the country club for a massage. I'll be finished by seven. Meet me in the dining room there for supper; just the two of us."

Before I could come up with an excuse, she hung up. Her words weren't a request, but an order.

I tossed the phone into my passenger seat and turned up my system. Shit was looking real good this way. I made another successful pickup yesterday. Instead of fifty bricks, the people had given me 200 this time. The good thing was that the work was the same raw product as last time. After cutting up the product, I issued Rah fifty and sent the rest to the stash house. Since our supply was so high, I made arrangements to meet my good friend Luis and his brother. Evidently, shit was still fucked up his way. They were supposed to come to the city to discuss business tomorrow. I was planning to make them an offer that they couldn't refuse.

* * * * *

(Rah)

"Where the fuck is this..." I mumbled to myself as my eyes scanned the crowded parking lot.

I spotted my people shortly and directed my girl to pull beside them. When Diamond pulled near the Crown Vic, her eyes caught the antennas and she kept pass it. I laughed to myself as I dialed Lt. Walsh's number to tell him that I had arrived.

"Baby, that's the law in that Vic," Diamond informed while circling the lot.

I directed her to park in a row over from the Vic, but in plain view so we could see who was inside. When Walsh came on the line, I directed him to my Escalade.

"There's an extra fifty in there just for you," I boasted after he was in my truck. He peeked into the bag and commented that my business must be good.

"Consider it a bonus and you can expect another bonus just like that around Christmas time as long as shit continues to run smoothly."

The look of greed in his eyes was priceless. The extra fifty was Prince's idea. He wanted to make sure that the goons stayed at bay so they could assure us no trouble. I had no problems with that. The money didn't come from my end anyway. If it was up to me, the greedy pig would be getting a bullet in the head instead of that hefty bag of money.

"Like I said before, you do your part and I'll do mine. And keep in mind that this is business and not personal. If it means anything to you, I've always liked you Rah," he said before stepping out of my truck.

I pointed Diamond in the direction of T.O.'s shop while I called Prince to tell him that the drop was made. He asked me did I handle that other business yet. He was speaking of the business ahead with T.O. I advised him that I was on the way at the moment and that I would call him later. Once I hung up, Diamond started asking questions.

"Please tell me that you just didn't give that police $150,000?"

She knew the contents of the bag because she counted it for me while I took a shower earlier. She was wifey, so I felt no need to keep secrets from her.

"You got to pay to play, baby," I stated while pulling a cigar from the glove box.

She studied the road before asking was shit back to normal on the streets; said she had noticed my grind and not to mention that I was on the way to my boy shop. So she was assuming.

"Shit is back to normal, but niggas' positions are different," I noted while kicking a Timberland up on the dash. "Let's just say that I've moved up from player to coach out here."

Before she could comment, we were pulling up on the lot. T.O. had a few customers out shopping and he was tending to one personally. Diamond and I got out and browsed while waiting. The boy T.O. had only exotic shit on his lot. Diamond stopped in front of a white CLK Benz and peeked inside.

"I like this one," she alerted proudly. "Put me in this and like Kanye West, 'you can't tell me nothing.'"

I inspected the whip further. The sticker stated that she was pre-owned with only 24K on the dash. T.O. was asking for fifty grand, but I knew I could drive it off the lot today for forty. It was about that time that I put shorty in her own wheels. This little coupe would complement my BMW perfectly.

T.O. swaggered over in all his glory. He mentioned something to me about a test drive, but never took his eyes off Diamond. He always checked out shorty as if he was undressing her with his eyes. I made a mental note to start coming to shop alone. A chick name Sandy suddenly appeared and provided a set of keys for Diamond. After she drove off, T.O. and I got down to business.

"You have good news for me," he asked immediately.

Me and Prince had already rehearsed my pitch and had agreed that with T.O. at the reigns, we could basically sit back and watch the money pile up.

"Shit is gravy my way. My people said that they are ready for whatever," I informed while looking inside a Maserati coupe.

"How's the quality," he questioned.

"Same good shit as before. Niggas was hitting that other shit three times and wasn't getting a complaint."

He nodded and asked what the tag was; said that he was expecting a good deal and for me not to come at him with that hundred grand price that I was taxing the streets. He told me that he was trying to sell weight, not get out there and sell the shit himself.

I winced before I spoke. Me and Prince had also discussed the price and had agreed to come down on it just enough for us to still see a nice profit and not hurt ourselves. With that in mind, I knew I had to stay in charge of the negotiations.

"Those fucking amigos are some greedy motherfuckers. You already know what they were taxing the last time and the price hasn't changed. I'm not making shit off the deal. I'm doing this on the strength of you," I lied.

T.O. shook his head. He said that it was no way that he could make any money if he was copping the shit for ninety a demo and then competing with me on the streets. After he finished ranting, he asked did I explain to them that he was trying to get over fifty; said that since he was spending so much, they should come down on the price.

"Yo T man, I told them motherfuckers all that. They are in control and know it," I told him with just enough attitude to let him know that it was a take it or leave situation.

He acted as if he was pondering my answer. Yo is a sharp dude and not to be underestimated. One didn't get as wealthy as him by being dumb. He finally asked were they planning to deliver. I told him that everything was on deck.

"Do I ever get to meet these amigos personally or should I expect business to keep taking place like this," he inquired.

"For right now, shit go through me, but I've already mentioned that in the future you would want to talk up for yourself," I lied.

Diamond pulled up and cut our conversation short. T.O. put his arm around my shoulder and escorted me back to the Benz. He asked Diamond if she liked the car.

"Do I like her," she asked sarcastically.

T.O. grinned, spoke into his walkie-talkie and told one of his employees to start getting the paperwork done on the Benz. Diamond gave me a look. I gave T.O. a look. For an answer, he told shorty that she could thank me for the car.

* * * * *

(T.O.)

It took me no more than an hour to get Rah and his girl squared away. No sooner than they drove off the lot, Diamond hit my phone up squealing. She was ecstatic.

"Thank you…thank you…thank you baby," she shrieked.

"It's nothing ma. I told you the other night before we left Vegas that I was gonna take care of you from that day forward," I reminded while remembering our pillow talk.

Either shorty was an actress deserving of an Oscar or she was just truly innocent. Baby girl brushed me off completely for the first two nights of our stay; complaining that she just wasn't ready. We stayed in the room together, slept in the same bed and all. I pulled every trick out the hat I knew, but she stuck to her guns. Finally, on our last night, I pulled out the big guns.

No stranger to the 'E' drug, I popped a pill and added a pill and a half to her drink. A bottle of Goose later and she was as loose as they come. Instead of wanting to be held that night, she wanted her pussy eaten. I happily obliged. Now that I think back, I probably wouldn't have fucked without the drugs that night. Instead of her resistance pissing me off, it actually turned me on. I'm just not used to females turning me down.

"How are you so sure that I bought the car," I asked curiously.

She popped her lips and said that if Rah would have copped it, the car would have been put in somebody else's name. She said that he was generous and all, but he just didn't believe in putting shit in her name; told me that that was his little way of trying to control her. I decided to turn the conversation in another direction instead of adding fuel to the fire.

"So when can I get a real personal thank you?"

Bruh entered my office then carrying a duffle bag. He pulled out a counting machine and got to work.

"Umm, I'm pretty sure that I can get loose tomorrow, but it's gonna have to be in the daytime while he's in the streets. I can't do that being out late again shit cause he might get suspicious," Diamond uttered.

Hearing her maneuver around old boy made me wonder if my wife Diane had ever moved around me like that. Shorty was far from a dummy and as headstrong as any woman I knew. Was she just accepting my shit all this time or was she doing her thing also. I had to shake those thoughts out of my head before I changed my mind about how generous I was being towards her concerning this divorce thing.

"I'm on your time Ma. You just call and I'll come running."

Bruh giggled and shook his head. Shorty said that she would get back at me with more details and we hung up. I turned to Bruh.

"Everything went as planned in D.C." I asked because I was getting a few complaints about my coke.

"Nigga wanted to know if the batch was different, but didn't argue once I dropped the price like you told me. I let him know that we were at the bottom of the barrel," he stated while rubber banding a ten thousand dollar stack. "We'll be off this shit by the time niggas are ready to re-up. Just make sure them Columbian niggas don't stick us again with this bullshit."

I nodded my head in agreement and told him about Rah's visit. I gave him the total rundown except the part about giving Diamond the car. His reply was that ninety a demo was real steep. He wanted to know how we were planning to make money also.

"Oh, we are definitely gonna make money," I said while leaning back in my chair. "It's still dry up and down these highways. I'm still getting calls from as far away as North Carolina. Selling the shit won't be a problem."

Bruh nodded his head; said that taking our show on the road wasn't a bad idea. He said we could leave B-more to the flunkies. I didn't like his statement. It was as if he was saying that we didn't still control the city. In truth, if we didn't get some work to compete with yo soon, that we could really kiss the city good bye. I'm not the one to accept defeat though.

"The nigga definitely got shit on smash right about now, but it's no way he can keep it for long. I got something for his ungrateful ass. We're gonna let him get his shine on for the time being," I told him.

* * * * *

Fresh

(Princess)

"Fuck it," I shouted to myself and then threw my cell phone to the floor.

The nigga J-Hood was the last nigga I had fucked and that was like a couple weeks ago. I had just dialed his number, plus another jump off out of DC, a couple of times and neither one of them niggas were answering. I grabbed the remote off my night table and hit the DVD player.

The nigga, Mr. Marcus, instantly came into view along with two other bitches. I grabbed my treasure box from up under my bed, picked my favorite rabbit clit tickler along with a sturdy vibrator out and climbed into my tub. On the screen, shit was moving along quite swiftly. Mr. Marcus was laid back on a recliner while watching the two bitches eat each other out.

Myself, I'm strictly dickly, but a little bi-curious on the low. I've never fucked another bitch. For the most part, I don't even like other bitches, period. I guess what I'm trying to say is seeing bitches on the screen turned me on a little, but I've never had an encounter.

Anyway, by the time Mr. Marcus was ready to join, I was almost at the point of no return. My cell rung and broke my concentration completely. My first thought was to ignore it, but thoughts of my jump off and the real thing made me reach for it. I answered without even looking at the caller ID.

"Hello?"

"Princess…" Hood said over the line.

I smiled on the inside, but copped an attitude because I was tired of his shit.

"Yo, you gonna make me fuck your ass up nigga. I been being nice, not wanting to hurt your little girlfriend feelings or whatever; but you keep playing with me and I'm gonna blow your spot up," I threatened.

He ignored the threats and told me that he needed me real bad. His voice sounded a little stained though.

"I need you too nigga. I'm sitting here in my tub…" I began but he cut me off.

"I'm serious Ma," he shouted and I got quiet. "Listen up real good because I really can't talk right now. I'm stranded out here in Jessup and these nice people are letting me use their phone. I lost mine and couldn't think of no other number to call but yours. I need you to come out here and get me right now."

I checked my caller ID and sure enough, he was not in the city. Any other time, I probably would've gotten smart and told him to call that bitch that he was so in love with to come get his ass. However, something in his voice told me not to ask questions and just go get him. I did have to ask if the police were chasing him though.

"No," he almost shouted again, but then calmed down. "Listen, just come get me now please."

I told him that I was on the way, got the address and stepped out the tub. Thirty minutes later, I was in Jessup. It took me another twenty minutes to find his ass and I was pissed.

When I finally pulled into the driveway of a nice neighborhood, Hood stepped onto the porch, looked both ways as if crossing the street and then dashed to my whip. I saw an older white dude shut the door behind him and shut off the porch light. In Hood's hands was a white shirt that was covered with blood.

"What in the hell are you into and why are you all the way out here," I asked after I pulled out.

He reached for a half a blunt that was visible in my ashtray, sparked it and then started giving me directions to get out of the boondocks. I stayed silent knowing that he would tell me what was up when he got ready. After ten minutes of driving and a couple of left turns, I spotted police lights ahead.

"Somebody must've heard the gunshots and called the damn law," he mumbled to himself.

I took the hint and pulled into the next driveway that I saw. I cut the lights, but not the engine. Hood was busy trying to see down the block. After a moment, he told me to take him to the city fast.

I was heated, but didn't act up. Instead, I merely backed out of the driveway and sped off in the opposite direction. When I found I-95, I started asking questions.

"Who in the hell lived back there? Why are you carrying that bloody ass shirt? Don't lie to me either, because once you got into my car, I became an accessory; so I at least need to know what's going on," I demanded.

He checked my ashtray for another blunt and didn't find one. I tossed him my Dior bag and a cigar from the armrest. After he got his blunt going, he was ready to talk.

"Me and shorty stay back that way. That was my house that the police was at," he stated nonchalantly. "Niggas robbed my crib tonight. They killed Sharon."

He got quiet and started to pull the blunt. I reached across and squeezed his hand. I was speechless also.

"I should've known something wasn't right when I pulled up. The damn garage door was up. Shorty would've never left it like that. I think that's how they surprised her. They were probably in the garage when she pulled up. Anyway, they ambushed me as soon as I came through the door. It was three of them.

One dude grabbed me. We tussled while the other two ran right pass me. One had a duffle bag and the other had a pillow case." He finally offered me the blunt. "Yo who I was tussling with wasn't trying to fight. Yo was trying to get away. I got his ass though…"

He pulled his gun from under his shirt and told me that he had shot old boy twice in the gut. He pointed to his bloodied shirt for an explanation.

"You said that they killed Sharon," I asked again.

Yo was hurt about that, I could tell. He shut his eyes. He seemed to be picturing everything over again in his head. I let him have his moment. After a minute, he wiped his eyes and sniffed.

"I found her upstairs in the bathtub. She had been drowned. The built-in safe under the floor boards of my bed was open. I had over two mill in there. They could've had the money though." He broke all the way down.

My mind was racing while he got it together. If shit went down as he said, it sounded as if he had a self-defense case. I told him my thoughts and mentioned that maybe we should go by my mother's house.

"I might could've gotten self-defense before, but after I found Sharon like that, I flipped out and hit yo up like eight more times in the head. He was trying to crawl out the garage."

He smiled as he said the last part. I started to question what state of mind that he was in, but he kept talking.

"I panicked though. After I did old boy, I ran. I left like five bricks back at the house that they probably didn't get. Shorty knew the combination to the safe, but she didn't know about the work."

He was thinking about work, but my mind was on that white dude whose house we had left. I asked who yo was and wondered if he was worried about him snitching.

"Oh, I know yo personally. Believe me, he can be trusted," he said as he rolled the window down and tossed all his evidence out the window. "That house that you picked me up from belonged to Joe Curry, that cracker that ran for Mayor in D.C. the last term."

I shook my head. I wasn't familiar with yo, but still concerned because yo had my number on his caller ID.

"Don't sweat that shit Ma. Yo ran for mayor but didn't win. Dude got a serious coke habit, and guess who his supplier is," he stated, sounding more like the cocky Hood that I'm used to. "If you say one word about me, I'll tell his little secret and he definitely don't want that."

By then, we were pulling into the city. I didn't even ask him where he wanted to be dropped off. I figured that he needed to go back to my crib with me so I could take his mind off of everything.

Chapter 7

(Gloria)

"Babe, could you get that for me," I yelled downstairs to Darius, who was near the front door.

I was expecting both of my kids, Pia and my nephew Raheem. After King asked me to organize his little operation to better protect our family, I got right on it and came up with a few ideas to wash up some of the money. Today was our first meeting of the minds. Darius came into my bedroom and kissed me on the neck.

"I'm about to head out. Your nephew is downstairs. Are you sure that you don't want any company tonight," he asked while getting a quick squeeze on my breast.

Ever since King's big announcement, my feelings for Darius had all but vanished. Yo is good people; a true gentleman. Not even King treated me like the Queen that Darius did. I cared for him a lot, but my heart and mind belonged to King. Now I had to figure out a way to break it off with Darius. King's pardon wouldn't be finalized until December. It's still early July, but I'm thinking that I should go ahead and break it off to give Darius the proper time to mourn the relationship. That way when Poppi comes home, it won't look like I deaded him on purpose.

"I'm good tonight. I have some work to do on the Baily case. I'll probably work into the wee hours. I'll just meet you at the club tomorrow for lunch," I said while closing the folder in front of me and preparing to walk him to the door.

Princess was coming thru the door as he was leaving. She was on her phone and didn't even bother to speak. After my meeting with King, I had met with Prince and got every detail of the operation out of him. Of course after I found out what roll my daughter was playing, I promptly called her and cursed her ass out too. We hadn't spoken since. I guess the hussy felt like the little fifty grand she was making made her independent. Before I could close my front door, I spotted Prince pulling up. A glance at my watch let me know that everyone was on time. I turned and headed towards the kitchen.

"I still can't believe yo did no shit like that," Rah was saying to Princess when I joined them in my kitchen. "It he's innocent, yo should just go talk to them."

"He's scared they are gonna lock him up." Princess' back was to me, but quit talking when she felt my presence.

It was time to lighten the mood. Rah was at my bar rolling a blunt. Normally, I would've popped him upside the head for even bringing the shit in my house, but instead, I merely picked up the bag, sniffed it and announced that they were about to smoke some 'Purple Hair Cess.' Rah looked at Princess and they both burst out laughing. I put my hands on my hips and glared at them.

"It's haze Aunt Glo; purple haze...But you was close," Rah said, then added. "What do you know about some Haze auntie?"

I merely shook my head and told them that what they were about to smoke was just what I said. The only difference was that the young people these days just changed the name like they did everything else. I almost started to explain, but the blank looks on their faces made it pointless. Instead, I went to my makeshift bar and started to pour drinks.

"I have a problem, Ma" Princess spouted as her brother and Pia entered the room. "I have a friend who may need to hire you."

In my sweetest voice, I told her that I was sorry to hear that, but I was gonna have to decline because I was already swamped at the office. After considering the state of our relationship lately, I changed my mind. I ended up telling her to have her friend call the office and I would get somebody to look at his problem. She glared at me to see if I was serious. After a second, she nodded and proceeded to greet her brother.

Fresh

I fixed Grey Goose for the boys and poured white wine for the ladies. After everyone took a glass and got comfy, I proceeded to make my proposal as if I was making a presentation to my partners at the firm.

"First of all, I would like to thank each of you for coming. It's a Friday night and everyone probably has plans; so I'll try not to take too much of your time." I then passed a folder to everyone.

"My son has asked me to help him somewhat organize his flourishing trade and though I don't agree with the trade itself, I've concluded that he's gonna do what he wants to anyway."

Out of the corner of my eye, I peeped the both Rah and Princess gave Prince. Per my request, I had told Prince not to tell them what this meeting was about. Trust played no part in my decision. My reason was because I needed the element of surprise. From the look that Rah had given Prince, I had succeeded.

` "With that said, since I can't beat him, I've decided to join him. Five heads together are better than one." This statement brought nods from everyone and lightened the mood. "Okay people; from what Prince has told me already, you guys' business is already pretty fool proof. It's only two minor adjustments that I think need to be made. Hear me our first and if you agree, then we'll see what we can do."

I got nods again and smiled to myself. This wasn't gonna be hard as I thought. I started by telling them that their business was pretty lucrative. In just over a month, it's made millions. There is no money like dope money, I must say so myself. But from my experience as a lawyer, the one mistake that the drug dealers of today make is their source of income. The pretty Benz that he drives... the condo by the harbor, etc.--all of that has to be accounted.

I took a second to glance around the room and deliberately let my eyes fall on Raheem last. He was basically the only real drug dealer in the room. The pretty condo in Federal Hill was evidence to the point. I told them that I couldn't let them make the same mistake that most people make. I pointed to the folders in front of them.

"In the folders I've distributed, you'll find several lucrative job descriptions that I've investigated. We should seriously think about divulging into these interests."

Everybody took the time to open their folders. I explained that each folder held different portfolios that maybe fitted everyone's lifestyle. Since Princess was into the whole club scene, her folder held promotional information, nightclub ownership documents and budget sheets. For Rah, I chose a clothing store. Since Pia was already set to get her real estate license this year, it was only right that she got the brokerage folder. For Prince, I wanted him to look into construction or something along those lines. To my surprise, Prince asked the first question.

"How am I supposed to get into construction when I'm supposed to go back to school next month?"

"I'm glad that you asked. As for construction, all you'll need to do is put in the ground work. If you look a little further, you'll see that the plan is for you to hire the proper contractors and basically let them run everything. That goes for basically everyone in the room."

I pointed at a list of certified people who had checked out to be capable of running such enterprises. Rah nodded his head. I tossed him a lighter and told everyone to turn the page.

"I've installed the proper business licenses and what not, that you'll all have to fill out to get things started. Either you can look for properties yourself or just hire agents. It really doesn't matter. I just want everyone's name down at the City Hall as business owners," I explained.

Princess still looked a little confused. Rah nodded and said that he understood completely. He explained to her that I was asking them to only get shit started, hire some people and probably make a few appearances. I nodded my head in agreement.

"I see that you're talking about promoting concerts at the Verizon Center and 1st Mariner Arena. This is big business you're talking about Ma," Princess noted.

"You're right and if you read a little further, you'll see plans to either open your own club or build one from the ground up."

"Build a club?" I saw Princess' eyes light up. "Where are we gonna get the money to build a club? And furthermore, promoting concerts means you need big names to sell them out. Entertainers are not cheap."

I told her that I understood and reminded her that I was far from stupid. She copped an instant attitude.

"Yo, I was just asking a question. Why do you always have to fix your voice in a condescending...?" She started but Prince cut her off.

He gave us both a look, and reminded us that we are here to put some goals together and not argue. I agreed and decided to move on with the meeting.

"Thanks to your brother, we have a budget of five million dollars to get all these plans off the ground. That will be more than enough money for what we are trying to do. As you can see, I've prepared a budget sheet and business plan."

Fresh

After the mention of so much money, I saw all eyes turn towards Prince. King had wanted to donate more, but didn't want to let on to Rah that Prince had mad more than him off of the last flip. I even noticed Pia's look which confirmed that he didn't tell her all his business. Prince noticed the looks and took the floor.

"Listen you guys, we all need to just open our minds and ears and listen. Five heads are better than one, remember." He scanned the eyes to makes sure they all agreed. "What we are trying to do is start something where everyone can make a good living and feel comfortable doing so."

I was amazed at the calmness of his voice when he spoke. He sounded like a boss; reminded me of his father for a minute.

"Pia, you've been quiet. Any questions or comments that you would like to add," I inquired.

"From what I see, you basically want to try to buy up a lot of these abandoned buildings around here, renovate them and resell. I see no problem with that. In fact, I think it's a good plan, especially with the marked the way it is these days. We'll save a lot of money from the recent foreclosures," she said as she flipped through the pages. "It might be hard trying to resell in some of the rougher neighborhoods though."

I nodded my head and reminded everyone that these were just preliminary goals and that we had plenty of time to put our heads together to plan better. Everyone nodded at my statement. Rah wanted to know how we would go about paying Prince back the money that he was investing.

"Phillips Incorporated will be our parent company. Each of you will be a subsidiary of that. You will own your company in name, but you will also be salaried employees. Of course, your salaries will be lavish enough to afford you a life of comfort. Over the years, our company will grow and prosper. You will all own shares in our corporation." I paused and looked around. "People this is only the beginning. Hopefully after you've gotten a taste of business, you'll grow and want to expand. It's a world of opportunity out there. It's our time to grasp it."

My little speech earned applause from all around the table. When all was settled, Princess asked about the proceeds from the drug operation. She wanted to know how they were being split.

King had only made a deal with his connection to deliver enough drugs to get him out and set him straight for future endeavors. Neither Prince nor Rah knew of his promise to stop after his release and I wanted to keep it that way. By the time the dope was gone, they would both be richer than they ever dreamed.

"Unfortunately, Prince and Rah will continue to share equally in that endeavor. They are putting in the majority of the work so it's only right," I said while looking at Rah to see his reaction. He looked relieved at the answer. "However, I'm hoping that as our businesses grow, we can convince them to leave that alone altogether."

* * * * *

(Rah)

As far as her comment about me quitting the game, she could forget it. Getting money is what I do. God put people on this earth for different reasons. I truly think that he put me here to get this money.

I peeped over in Prince's direction to see how he was taking her little quitting speech. It didn't surprise me that he was actually nodding his head and agreeing with her. Seeing him agree like that made me want to stack my chips tight and prepare for a rainy day because it was obvious this guy wasn't built like me. Hopefully, if he decided to quit, I could convince him to hand the plug over to a real nigga.

As for the rest of Aunt Glo's plans, I was all for it. I see nothing wrong with getting some legal money. In fact, I had wanted to get something legit going for a while. It would only help me keep the people off my back and since she wanted to help me out, I decided to lay back and listen for the remainder of the meeting.

As the conference winded down and everyone prepared to leave, Aunt Glo asked me to stay over for a minute. I called Diamond while she let everyone else out. It was after midnight and thankfully she was asleep. Since she was tucked in for the night, I decided to text my jump off, Kim, and see if I could swing through. Aunt Glo handed me a fresh drink when she returned and sat down beside me. She asked me how I felt about her proposal tonight.

I chose to be real careful with my answer. Something told me that she was after something else. After all, Aunt Glo is far from a dummy. Not only was she book smart, but she had street sense too.

"I'm all for everything Aunt Glo. I was especially interested in the part about the corporation. With us combining our businesses, we have no other choice but to make money," I stressed to let her know that I was paying attention earlier.

She studied me for a long moment and finally nodded her head. When she spoke she told me that she loved me as if I was hers and wanted me to know that she didn't see me any different from Prince. In other words, she was telling me that she had my best interest in mind at all times.

Fresh

"I know Auntie and I wanted to thank you again for what you did during that situation..."

She stopped me in my tracks; told me that this talk wasn't about what happened to me and Prince. After seeing that I understood, she went on to explain that this talk was about me being smart and handling the streets with as much caution as possible. She told me that we were in enough trouble as is and couldn't afford anymore slips, especially with the endeavors that we were about to undertake.

I knew exactly what she was getting at and was about to explain but my phone cut me off. It was my jump off, Kim, letting me know that I was more than welcome to stop through her crib tonight. Aunt Glo noticed the grin on my face and exhaled.

"Listen, I know you're on top of your shit. I'm just warning you to be more careful. If you're dealing with three lieutenants, narrow it down to two. Put layers between you and the streets to make it harder for the authorities to catch up with whose really in control. Protect yourself, son. Always keep in mind that one loose brick causes the fall of the entire house and you know what I'm talking about," she said before getting up to escort me out.

In my car on the way to the city, I thought about what my aunt had just run down and decided to take heed. Columbian drug lords survived so long because they kept a certain chain of command separating them from the streets. Then I thought of T.O. and how he ran his organization. I had been dealing with yo for years and couldn't think of one time that I had actually received drugs from him personally or paid him money in his own hands. Dude dealt with only a selected few and never on the phone. Those were his rules and niggas respected that shit too. Yeah, he was a cautious motherfucker and a free motherfucker also, which was more than I could say for a lot of Kingpin niggas I has seen come and go through Baltimore.

* * * * *

(Prince)

I woke up the next morning by myself. The house was silent, which was a pleasant surprise. I yelled down to Pia to see if I was really alone. She responded that she was in the kitchen and wanted to know if I wanted any breakfast. I headed to the restroom to get myself together. What I really wanted was some early morning loving and decided to make a play for it while on my way to the kitchen.

Shorty was at the kitchen table going through the folder mom had presented to her last night. She was so excited about the meeting that I received the royal treatment that's only reserved for my birthday. I went over and kissed her neck.

Fresh

"It's too early to be going through that shit. Why don't you come back up so we can finish where we left of last night," I whispered to her.

She slid out of my grasp and headed for the fridge. She stated over her shoulder that I couldn't have any. Before I asked why, she informed that I had knocked her period on with that rough stuff.

I shook my head and headed for the back door. I wanted to see how it felt outside. The sun was up and the birds were chirping. It was gonna be a good day. Pia started talking some shit about how she felt it was better to target some of the recent foreclosures around Baltimore. I mumbled that whatever she chose to do was perfectly fine with me and headed back for the stairs. I guess she thought that I was pissed about her period because she stepped in my way and wrapped her arms around me.

"Are you mad?" She reached for my wood and started to lower to her knees. "It's still other things that I can do, you know."

I raised an eyebrow to tease. Shorty wasn't big on giving head, which was the reason I was so sprung on Quita. For some reason, I wasn't in the mood for her attempts this morning so I stopped her.

"Let's go to the New York and shop," I suggested out of the blue.

She rose back to her feet and asked me what I was talking about. I repeated myself and stated that I wanted to fly up to New York today to do some shopping. I was sitting on a bunch of cash, hadn't spent a dime and was in the mood to splurge some. She gave me a long stare and then smiled. She agreed that going out of town didn't sound bad at all.

* * * * *

(T.O.)

"Shit!"

I almost reached for my gun when I heard the scream. Diamond jumped out of bed and started to frantically look for her clothes. Sunlight was shining through the drapes and I groaned.

"I'm fucked up...I fucked up...Oh damn, I'm fucked!" She scolded herself before pointing an accusing finger at me. "And, it is your fault!"

I frowned and started to get out of bed. I told her to watch her tone when speaking to me.

"I'm not watching shit! It really is your fault. I tried to leave last night, but you begged me to stay," she recollected as she tried to put on her bra.

I couldn't protest. It really was my fault why she spent the night. Shorty had stopped through the club last night unannounced. After we had gotten tipsy, I had Bruh drop us off at my penthouse in

Butcher's Hill. We fucked long and hard. By midnight, she was ready to make her exit, but I persuaded her to hop back on top for one final ride. Now, it was daylight and she was in a lot of trouble. After she was half decent, she made a beeline for my front door but stopped once she realized her car was still parked at the club.

"Fuck," she yelled in frustration. "Can you...better yet, I'll call a cab."

I proceeded to get dressed patiently while she went through the motions. When I was ready, I informed her that I would have given her a ride if she wanted one. She accepted. Ten minutes later, we were in my Porsche on the way to her car. She busied herself calling alibis while I concentrated on the road. From the sound of her conversations, it seemed as if she was in trouble already.

"Bad news," I asked after her first call.

"Hell yeah," she snapped. "That was my mother. She said that he's called her three times already. And I know that he's probably already called my sister as well, but I still have to try!"

It didn't sound as if she had much luck with her sister either. I heard her sister loud and clear. As hysterical as she sounded, you would think that she was in trouble. Before she could make another call, her phone rang in her hands. She looked at the caller ID and started to literally cry.

"Oh God, this is him. I can't answer this."

She was looking at me as if I had some answers. I merely shook my head. After the call ended, she tried to Irene and learned that he had called there too. She finally asked what she was supposed to do after she hung up.

"Keep calling people. A cousin out of the city, but close, would probably work," I advised.

"Rah know I don't fuck..." She stopped in mid-sentence as if she suddenly had a bright idea and started dialing.

By the time I pulled up to her Benz, she had made contact with a cousin in PG County. Before I could even stop the car, she was out the door. I couldn't even get in a parting word. After she pulled off, I called Bruh and told him to meet me at the club. He showed up thirty minutes later, freshly scrubbed and looking rejuvenated. I locked up my Porsche and hopped in the Maybach with him.

"I got some fast and easy money for you to make if you're interested," were the words I spoke to Bruh.

"I'm listening," he replied.

First, I ran down the situation that had just transpired between me and Diamond. I told him since Rah would obviously have his mind on other things, it would be a good idea to apply some pressure to his ass. Bruh agreed like he usually does when I present these master plans to him. He told me to tell him what I wanted done.

"The way I see it is old habits are hard to break. With that in mind, I'm willing to bet that the stash situation is still the same."

Bruh started to nod his head, no doubt catching on to what I was getting at. Yo wasn't a dumb dude by far. He had learned a lot from me over the years. I made my pitch.

"Use Lil' Thug and them out of VA to put in the work. Y'all split the money however you see fit. And I suggest that you get on this today while his mind is still elsewhere."

* * * * *

(Princess)

It's only been one week since I got that crazy call from Hood and he's been holed up in my crib ever since. I'm used to my own space, but couldn't gather the nerve to kick him out, so I came up with another plan.

He was in a tight situation. His only family in B-More was his grandmother and he was sure that the police would look there first. Every so called friend he was dealing with decided to get amnesia when he dialed their number. The grimy niggas that hustled for him took his bad fortune as an opportunity to go for self. To make a long story short, he was just all in and assed out.

To make matters worse, I was about tired of him. As bad as I hate to admit it, the boy is one of my weaknesses. Too much of what he had in his pants does things to a woman. It's only been a week and I'm under his spell already. I'm just sad to say that as much as I used to crave his attention, now I think I'm getting too much of it.

The other reason it was time for him to move on was because this is not my apartment to myself. My mother rented this place and paid the bills for me and Twin. She also had keys to the joint. It would be just my luck that she came waltzing in one day to find me harboring a fugitive.

All this led to the events and decisions that I had just made. Hood's original plan was to head down south where he had a cousin that was ready to take him in. He was all for it but was determined not to make the move broke. I offered to give him a loan, but the little bread that I could offer wouldn't do him any good. Yo wanted to make a move and was plotting to kidnap his right hand man to come up with the proper funds. After hearing his plans, I knew I had to help out before he somehow involved me.

With that in mind, I made the drive to Jessup and chipped an ounce off the last fourteen bricks that Prince had left. Yeah, it was a grimy thing to do, but Rah was moving the shit so fast that he probably wouldn't notice. When I returned back home, I woke Hood with a kiss and a squeeze to his manhood.

Fresh

"That's what's up Ma," he said with a moan. "I could get used to waking up like this every morning," he stated while reaching for me.

I moved out of his grasp and reached for a Macy's bag that I had placed on the floor. After handing it to him, he instantly emptied the contents on the bed and gave me a curious glare while examining the heroin before him. Before I could explain, he asked me where I had gotten it from. I noticed that he was busy tearing into the package as he asked. So I smiled.

"It really shouldn't matter where I got the shit from," I stated while crawling seductively back into his lap. "You said that you didn't like being broke, so I took the necessary steps to put some money in your pocket."

I started to plant light kisses on his tattooed chest. As I moved lower, he pulled me back up to his face and stuck his tongue down my throat. In no time, he had taken control of the situation. Any other time, I would have loved to let him dominate the pussy, but this moment was about business. I moved out of his grasp again and produced an envelope from my purse.

"I went by the bank this morning and got you some money. It's only five grand but I figure it's enough to get you down south and started. I guess I can make the trip down there after you're settled and on your feet." I bent my head to kiss his hardening dick, and asked him what he thought.

* * * * *

(Prince)

As soon as we hit the Big Apple, our first stop was to the diamond district. Pia isn't big on jewelry herself, but I've been a fanatic since the tender age of fourteen. The first store we his was called 'Diamonds Are Us' and I was in heaven. It was so much ice in that joint that it didn't even need an air conditioner.

The first piece that caught my eye was a pair of five carat ear rings. From the first glance, I could tell that they were flawless. The jeweler saw me peeping them and came over with a lope and white towel to show their authenticity. I could see straight through them shits. I asked the Arab how much he wanted.

"The tag says thirteen, but if we are talking cash then I'm sure something can be worked out," he answered.

He reached for a calculator while I moved down the display. I spotted a smaller identical set of rings and thought of Asia. I told Pia that I was gonna get them.

"Prince, those are too much for Asia. What if she loses them on the playground or something," she scolded.

Fresh

I ignored her and moved over to the chains and bracelets. Didn't much catch my eye over there except a platinum dog tag with the iced out tag. I turned to the jeweler.

"Add both of those tags, the chain and this smaller set up with that. And do you think that you can engrave hers' and my daughter's name into the tag today," I asked.

The Arab wiped his brow and started to stutter. All of this talk and no was in sight. Yo was probably suspicious that I was gonna rob him. To ease his mind, I took the Gucci book bag from Pia and flashed him the stacks that were inside. He instantly told me that he could have the names engraved by the next morning. I nodded and turned to Pia.

"You see anything that you like?"

She pointed to a watch that I didn't even notice; said she liked it, and it was hers. The Arab was on his job and quickly announced that he had the watch in his and hers set. I bit. We ended up in his office to work out the final details. I spent over forty grand with his ass.

We hailed a cab outside the store and proceeded to the garment district. Pia commented on how much I had spent and told me to slow down.

"Listen Ma, we came to have a good time and that's what I intend to do. We're going first class all the way this weekend," I boasted.

"I understand that and I appreciate the watch, but now I wish that you would've gotten me a car instead of a watch that I don't plan to wear every day."

Shorty drove a three year old Honda Civic these days. It was definitely time for an upgrade. And while my mind was on cars, I started to think of one for me.

"We're gonna make that happen for you as soon as we get back to the city," I said as she jumped into my arms.

We pulled in front of the Gucci boutique and the cabbie stopped. Up further, I saw a Prada, Jimmy Choo and Fendi store. I thought of Twin and how at home she would feel on this strip. With that in mind, I reached into our book bag and produced two ten thousand dollar stacks.

"Go have a good time Ma. I'm gonna go find us a hotel to check into. Buy something sexy for a nigga. I guess we can find a club to party at tonight."

Of course she whined about me leaving her, but let me off the hook because she knew I hated shopping with females. As soon as she was out of the cab, I told the driver to circle the block and drop me at the Louis Vuitton store. Wasn't no way I could come to New York and forget about Quita. We had done some light texting while I was on the plane. She told me to scoop her up a nice bag or something. I ended up dropping six grand on her ass and having her stuff shipped to Baltimore.

I left there and headed to Time Square to find a nice hotel. The cabbie took the long route and even tried to jip me out of my change by claiming my bill was too large. Right when I was about to curse his African ass out, a familiar face came strolling out of the hotel with a pretty little white girl on his arm. I smiled to myself, lifted my phone and snapped a few pictures of my mother's fiancé.

* * * * *

(Raheem)

Diamond came into the den and sat my dinner in front of me. I was involved in a game of Call of Duty and didn't even glance at the food. I could smell it though, but still refrained. As hungry as I was, I couldn't eat. My stomach was literally upset and had been like that since shorty came waltzing her ass in here this morning. I had all her shit packed and ready for her ass too. A bitch cheating on me is unacceptable; especially the female that I've chosen to wife. Her ass was out and she wouldn't be here in front of me now if she didn't give a good alibi.

Her excuse was that she over her cousin's Angie's house out in PG County. They ended up going to a club and getting fucked up. She even showed me a faded out stamp on her hand to prove that she'd been at a club. When I asked why she didn't call, she explained that she had lost her phone. She said that she got tore up and they ended up leaving the club early; claimed that she wound up on her cousin's couch last night. Of course, her cousin vouched for her, which left a little sympathy in me.

After rationalizing, I can say that shorty don't fuck with too many bitches. I thought I had all the bases covered, but had totally forgotten about Angie. If something was indeed not right, I couldn't point a finger at it, which left me to let her off with a stern warning. Her voice snapped me out of my thoughts.

"Your food is getting cold."

"I'm not in the mood to eat right now," I replied.

She was on her feet in an instant. With her hands on her hips, she started to complain about her cooking and me not wanting to eat. She was so timid at times that it always turned me on to see her pissed off. The shit wasn't working this time though. I halted the game and headed for the bedroom. As I was getting dressed, she went for my phone and asked who Kim was. I gave her a glare.

"Who the fuck is Kim, motherfucker and why is she texting you about dinner," She yelled with attitude.

Fresh

I was busted, but didn't miss a beat. Another reason I wasn't in the mood for her food was because my jump off Kim was busy getting me the same meal ready. Earlier, I had merely mentioned that I was hungry and Diamond took it upon herself to cook for me. Little did she know I was busy texting Kim to do the same thing. Tired of me ignoring her, she threw the phone at me.

"Oh, so you're gonna ignore me now?"

"What the fuck is you talking about girl," I questioned as I went to get my jewels together.

"Oh, I'm crazy now? Here is another text from the bitch; this morning at 12:33 a.m. 'Yeah, I'm up. You can come through.' Motherfucker..."

I turned around and snatched my phone from her grasp. I told her not to try to turn things around on me because she fucked up. I grabbed my keys and brushed pass her. She hopped in my way.

"I'm a grown ass man Diamond! I come and go when I please," I reminded her.

She was on my back instantly; punching and screaming. I stumble near the bed and hip tossed her on the mattress. Never have I put my hands on her, but tonight it was different. I slapped her twice just to get her attention.

"Bitch, you better never put your hands on me again!" She screamed and started bawling like a baby.

I headed out the door. When I made it to my car, I decided against going to Kim's just yet and called Gutta. I still hadn't turned the reigns over to him and Murder yet. Tonight would be a good time to set those wheels in motion.

"Man, I was just about to dial your number. You need to come through Winchester now," he said when he answered.

I informed him that I was on the way and took a deep breath. The only tie that I had to Winchester Apartments was Nita's house. Shorty was an old friend that I grew up with. I used her house these days as a stash spot. The boys went by to drop cash and re-up when work was needed. My instincts told me that something bad had happened.

I called Murder as I drove to see what he knew. As usual, he was at the spot putting in work and didn't know shit. I told him to meet me out Winchester anyway.

When I made it to the apartments, Murder's Yukon was already there. I instantly tapped into my secret compartment to get my 40 out. When Murder opened the door to let me in, I almost threw up. The living room was ransacked. Everything was turned over. Straight through the kitchen, I could see Nita tied to a chair with her throat slit from ear to ear.

"We out of like a half a mill man. I had made four drops already today," Murder said. "The nigga Gutta said that he had been through like six times himself. How much work was over here?"

I heard him but really wasn't hearing him. The toilet in the bathroom flushed. Gutta came out and handed me a Ross bag. I instantly reached into my dip, pulled out my joint and put three in his chest. He was dead before he hit the ground. Murder jumped back. I put the gun back into my dip and let him know that everything was okay.

"We've been operating out of these apartments for over two years now. All of a sudden we start fucking with this clown and..." I let my words trail off.

Murder, starting to read my mind, only nodded. On the drive over I had already tried and convicted Gutta. If he wasn't guilty, then I would just let this be a lesson to the streets. I snatched up my bag of money.

"Promote that nigga Moneybags to lieutenant of your shop. I want you to go over to Pennsylvania Ave. to take over." I headed for the door before stopping. "Come back here before daylight and torch the place. I'll contact you tomorrow with details on a new stash spot."

Chapter 8

(Princess)

"Girlll…I swear, your brother better not try to play me tonight or I'm gonna act a fool," Quita announced as she applied the finishing touches to my makeup.

I heard her, but my mind was elsewhere. Inside, I'm all giddy and shit. Now I can relate to how a bride must feel on her wedding day. Too bad I'm not getting hitched though. Still, tonight is my night, and all this bitch can do is whine about my brother.

'Princess's Palace' is scheduled to open tonight. I rented a property on D.C.'s waterfront to set up shop. True, Baltimore is in serious need of a good club, but my city could never work for the type of club I envisioned. My shit is an ultra-club, big enough to accommodate a thousand people. With that in mind, it's only right that I open up in the D.C. area.

'Love Nightclub' had already set the standards and was my main competition. After hiring a top notch PR firm for publicity, I set my sights on getting some entertainment to attract partygoers. With that in the bag, I made the power move of stealing Love's manager to come work his magic at my spot.

The whole club and business plan was expensive but I got no complaints from my mother. She was just ecstatic that I was putting things down and didn't bat an eye when I needed money. We came to the conclusion that the club would start to turn a profit in record time.

The scent of sour diesel hit my nostrils and took me out of my thoughts. I stood to inspect my gear for the night. Not wanting to overdo the regular folk, I chose a black Yves Saint Laurent mini jump off with some opened toed Christen Louboutin heels. My jewels for the night were borrowed from my mother's jewelry box. My ears held 4 carats all together. Around my neck, I sported a diamond choker. My wrist and ankle held matching bracelets.

My girl Quita was not bullshitting either. Instead of the high fashion look, she chose a Fendi sweater that doubled as a dress, some leggings and ankle boots. Her hair was puffed out in a natural and her arms were filled with bangles. She was on point and ready to go. I decided to put her in her place before we left and let her know that I didn't want any shit out of her and Prince.

"I'm just saying, you already know Pia gonna be there, so it's only so much the boy can do," I advised.

She rolled her eyes and popped her lips. She said it was too many fish in the sea for her to sweat one. With that said, she put on her Fendi specks and we headed out to the stretch Hummer that I had rented for the night. Quita grabbed two glasses from the bar and poured us some Cristal. After handing me mines, she produced two X-pills, but I declined. Any other night I would have gotten crunk, but tonight was too important. I needed to be on point for real. She tossed hers back anyway. I immediately teased her that she would definitely get horny tonight and Prince would probably be too occupied to help her out.

"Please! If I want that tonight, trust, I can get it. But on the real, I'm not even gonna stress your brother tonight. Believe me, I have 99 problems, but a nigga isn't one," she responded.

I gave her a high five and decided to text my booty call for the night. The event was too important for me to sleep alone. With that out of the way, we made small talk until we finally pulled up to a line as long as the welfare office.

"Let me find out that T.I. really brought them out," Quita teased, referring to our guest performer for the night.

The driver stopped the Hummer right at the front door. All eyes were on the Hummer as if T.I. was about to step out. I noticed how salty bitches looked when the driver opened the door and we exited. We walked straight to the front. The bouncer quickly removed the rope to let us in. I commented on the full house as we entered.

"We're almost to capacity. Oz told me to slow down and try to get more VIP's," the bouncer told me.

Oz was the brains that I had stolen from our competition. The admission price tonight was forty bucks and two hundred for VIP booths. I looked at the women standing in line, all dressed to impress. They reminded me of back in my club hopping days. Most had probably gone shopping just for tonight. I got soft and turned to the bouncer.

"Start letting these ladies in," I said while winking at the first few in line.

* * * * *

(T.O.)

Instead of Bruh picking me up from the airport, I found the roles reversed this time. Tonight, I had the duty of picking him up. I spotted him as he strolled out the terminal nonchalantly and blew the horn. He jumped in and we stayed quiet until we were safely on the beltway.

"Everything's a go. The shit will be here in less than 48 hours. The Africans send their regards."

I smiled and nodded my head. The African he was talking about was an old connection out of Louisiana that I used to deal with before the drought hit. Yo had just gotten back in power and Bruh had went to see him. The prices were right and his product was always on point. I just hoped it was good enough to stand up to the shit that Rah was selling.

"So what's the plan," Bruh asked, probably aware that I already had one in place.

I asked how much of the other shit did we have left. He confirmed that we still had about 40 bricks of uncut. I thought about that before making my decision.

"Contact V-Skee and Boss from Park Heights. Also holler at Pollaye and Styles. Tell them niggas that we are back in power. When you hit the kitchen, mix that uncut with the new shit and see what happens," I instructed.

He nodded while looking through his phone. I asked him did we have any vacant rental property on Brice St. available. He confirmed that we were all booked in that section.

"Find replacement housing for all the tenants over there. Offer free moving fees and one month's free rent for the inconvenience. Tell them we are about to do some renovating. I want everything cleared out in two weeks."

Bruh never questioned me but I could tell that my request bothered him by the look in his eyes. The boy Raheem had two shops around the corner from that area. He asked me did I plan to move on old boy. I just smiled. Old boy knew me way too well.

* * * * *

(Rah)

Diamond canceled on me at the last minute, claiming the flu. The only other bitch I had worthy of accompanying me to Princess's club tonight was Kim, but she was out of town. Not wanting to be alone tonight, I ended up calling Murder to shut down the shop and bring the boys out on me.

With that said, we loaded up the SUV's and headed for D.C. Thirty six niggas in all, we crowded the door ready for whatever. Seeing all of us, we were immediately frowned upon. I had to call Princess to the front door just to get admitted in.

Princess directed me and my team straight to a VIP booth opposite T.I. and his entourage. I spotted Prince and Pia posted at the rail looking out at the club and went to holler. It was my first time seeing the club personally and I had to admit that Princess had done an excellent job. Prince agreed and then whispered that he needed me to run interference so he could go holler at Quita. I told him that I would do it and he slipped me a key to Princess's office.

I left him and took in the sights. Princess had three bars set up; two in the VIP section and one on the main floor. I spotted Quita and Princess in T.I.'s personal booth and strolled over. Of course his security stopped me, but Princess let them know that I was all good. T.I. had his arm around Quita chatting her up when I sat down. Princess made the introduction. Yo stood up to greet me. I liked that. It showed that he was still a regular dude. I leaned in close to whisper to Quita.

"Prince wants you to meet him in the office in fifteen," I told her as I handed the key to her.

Evidently T.I. didn't hold any weight because she quickly grabbed the key and disappeared. As soon as she left, Princess got the camera man's attention and we took some flicks. I'm not a star struck nigga myself, but felt the pictures would be good to hang in the clothing store that I was planning to open in the Galleria mall.

After the pictures were complete, T.I. excused himself to hit the stage. I stayed grounded and surveyed the scene. On the dance floor, I spotted two of the finest females in the building. One was tall dark skinned and reminded me of the model Selita Ebanks. The other one was short and thick like the Kardashian chick, but reminded me of Cassie. She must've felt my eyes on her because she caught me staring and held my glance before turning to the stage area. I got Princess' attention, pointed in the female's direction and asked did she know them. She took one glance and started shaking her head in the negative.

"Oh, it's nothing Cuzzo. That ain't nothing but trouble over there," she stated. Then she asked did I know Baby Ray.

I nodded that I had heard of old boy but never met him. Rumor was that he was a big time nigga out of D.C. Yo was supposed to have the coke game on lock around these parts. I had seen him at T.O.'s shop copping a Ferrari once. I stood to approach shorty, but Princess pulled me back to my seat.

"I'm telling you that the bitch is nothing but trouble, but I know you. Anyway, just be careful. Plenty of niggas have gotten in beef behind shorty. Don't fall victim," she warned.

I looked back at shorty. The partygoers were all headed to the stage area. Old girl stood back and looked on at one of the big screens that Princess had displayed in the club. I moved in her direction. I caught up with them at the bar and stopped shorty before she could pay for the drinks she ordered.

"Oh no, I can't let you do that. Your money is like counterfeit when I'm in the building. I got to pay for everything," I related as I slid in the seat next to her and pulled out my bankroll.

"Well, in that case, take these glasses back and hand us a bottle of Cristal," she told the bartender who promptly looked at me for my approval.

"You heard the lady. Get her the Cris' and I'll have a bottle of that Goose."

I kept eye contact with shorty as I peeled off the C-notes to pay the bill. The bartender slid a bucket and two glasses to them before disappearing to get my bottle.

"Thanks for the bottle, cutie," she flirted with a wink before trying to disappear.

I reached for her arm and introduced myself. Instead of telling me her name, she gave me a disappointed look. The bitch acted as if I should have known her name so I repeated myself. Shorty burst out laughing.

"I can't believe that you don't remember me Raheem Phillips," she added before poking her lip out. "Shanika Cartwright...Bootsie's little sister. We were in elementary together. Remember Miss Hawkins' class when you beat up Tim Rankins for spitting on me."

Shanika Cartwright... Bootsie's little sister...Miss Hawkins...None of that rang a bell. It was the comment about the fight with Tim that I did remember.

"Little Nika...," I said while pulling her in for a hug. "Damn, it's been years. You're gorgeous!"

Fresh

"I know right," she winked while giving me a little spin. "You're looking good yourself."

I tried to pull her in for another hug but she resisted. I thought about what Princess had told me and backed away. Instead of beating around the bush, I went straight for the kill and asked for her number. She shook her head and told me that she couldn't do it, but did mention that she owned a shop in the Georgetown area that specialized in bags. She told me that I should come buy my girl a bag.

* * * * *

(Prince)

"If it ain't one thing it's a motherfucking 'nother," I mumbled to myself as I tossed my phone into the passenger seat. It seems like I've had the bad luck blues lately. Two months ago I got booted from Penn State. They claimed that I would be reinstated once my legal troubles were settled.

If that wasn't enough to drive a young man crazy, Quita hit me with a blow designed to cripple me. Shorty was claiming pregnant. Of course we got into a screaming match. I said some things that I shouldn't have said and she countered with some inappropriate shit. But today on this drive to see my pops, I had time to think. This baby didn't ask to be here and I had no business telling shorty to abort.

With that said, I was just gonna find a way to tell Pia and deal with her wrath.

As usual, it took pops an hour to get out on the visiting floor. He looked stressed. I saw bags under his eyes as if he hadn't been getting the proper rest. That surprised me. If I was in his position, I would've been kicked back, letting the days go by. He had no reason whatsoever to be worried. His get out of jail free pass was already bought and paid for. We were just waiting on the new President so we could get this show on the road.

"What's up with you man," I asked as he took his seat.

He put his face into his hands. After a minute, he revealed his red eyes. Something was definitely up. I asked him again what the problem was.

"We have a problem son," he admitted.

I told him that he could talk to me about anything. After a long moment, he scooted closer and started whispering. He started by telling me that he had a favor to ask of me. He stated that if I denied him this favor, then all was good; said the only reason he was even asking me was because of the sensitivity of the matter. I got tired of guessing and told him to just spill it. He took a deep breath and started from the beginning. He repeated the history of the get out of jail scam. Then he ended by telling me about this big shot Senator who had it in for the sitting President. He asked have I ever heard of the dude.

"Senator O'Reilly," I replied and shook my head. "You said that he's out of Texas, right?"

Pops nodded. He said that the senator was a Republican from Texas that's been after our President since day one. He mentioned that the rumor was that he was trying to launch a big corruption investigation aimed at the White House. He said that the pardon hadn't been brought up, but since the President had gotten wind of the investigation, he wasn't too excited about pardons. I stopped him in his tracks.

"That's some bullshit man. We already delivered payment to those people. What..."

He cut my statement short. He stated that he knew what was good but that the President was just a little paranoid of this Senator dude. He was looking me in the eyes as he spoke. I was starting to get where he was coming from. I decided to ask what was on his mind.

"So you're saying that the President won't move on this thing unless this Senator dude either backs off or pulls a disappearing act. Either or..."

For an answer, he nodded. Then he said that the latter would be more assuring for everybody. He had a pleading look in his eyes. I sat back and exhaled. The wheels in my head started turning. Finally, I asked exactly what he needed me to do.

* * * * *

(Gloria)

'Baltimore Lawyers Sue State Police' was the caption on the front page of the Baltimore Sun.

'State Police Accused of Racial Profiling on I-95' was what the Washington Post stated.

I read both articles and smiled to myself. Pulling this off had been easy. After showing my partners the statistics of the black people being pulled over on I-95 for no reason, they quickly gave me their blessing. A little donation to my friends at both papers bought me full court front page pressure. This case against my son would have to be won in the media. Well, with that and a few other crafty tricks that I had up my sleeve.

I sat in my home office trying to concentrate on the work in front of me, but couldn't get King out of my mind. Preparations for his homecoming were on my agenda also. I had contacted a few travel agencies to put a month long vacation in the works. Today's work load involved Prince though. On my desk, I had everything that Johnny could dig up on the enemy.

Both the judge and prosecutor appeared to be in order. The same went for the arresting officer except he had a thing for Atlantic City and roulette tables. However, the other arresting officer was another story. Officer Ryan Frye was the officer sitting in his car during the arrest. According to Johnny's report, Officer Frye's job performance was impeccable. However, his home life was something else. He was married to the daughter of Elkton's Mayor. He and his wife shared a child who was diagnosed as being Autistic. While wifey spent all of her free time attending to the child, Officer Frye spent his laid up with his mistress here in Baltimore. The kicker was that his mistress was black.

Sensing that I would be interested, Johnny went ahead and did his homework on the mistress. It turns out that Miss Tiffany Allen is a stripper at one of the city's more exclusive clubs. For extra money, she wasn't above turning a trick or two. Of course, Officer Frye knew nothing of this extra hustle. To him, she was an aspiring model who worshipped the ground that he walked on. Of course he paid handsomely for this luxury.

After reading all of this, I gave Johnny the go ahead to approach shorty with twenty five grand to allow us to set up a camera and listening device in her bedroom with hopes of accumulating some incriminating evidence to hold over his head. We had no reason to believe that she wouldn't comply, but in case she didn't we were prepared to offer fifty stacks.

I sat all the files aside and wiped my eyes. My watch said that it was a quarter 'til eight. I stretched, got up and decided to go get ready for my date. It was time to break off my engagement with Darius.

Fresh

Chapter 9

(Raheem)

It turns out that opening 'The Spot', my men's clothing store was a good idea. Going for a diverse clientele, I ended up renting a space at the mall. The store was an ex Rite-Aid and had plenty of space. I packed the place with every hot clothing line I could think of. I sold everything. For the hip hop crowd, I carry everything from Coogi to Iceberg. For the professional shoppers, I carried Armani casual wear and Hugo Boss suits. My store also had a children's section to keep the youngins fly.

I employed five females to cater to the male shoppers and five male employees to grasp the ladies attention. Of course, Diamond wanted to get involved so I appointed her to manage the joint. She was doing such a good job that I was already plotting to open a women's store next door for her.

When I first started putting the store together, I had no intentions of actually working the place. But since the place opened, I just can't seem to stay away. I'm a hustler by nature. It doesn't matter if I'm selling heroin or clothes, I can sell the shit. And that's exactly what I was doing when Nika waltzed her pretty ass in my store. I quickly handed the customer in front of me his change and approached her at the cologne section.

"If I may suggest something, I think the Burberry is magnificent." I leaned in so she could catch a whiff of the fragrance on me. "It smells fruity and sweet, yet it's light on the nose."

She burst out laughing and said that she liked the professional voice. She glanced around my store and nodded. She complimented that she liked how big and spacious it was. She joked that it made her store look like a shack.

I had stopped by her shop as she suggested. She had a decent little operation going; one that catered to hand bags. Any Gucci bag that you could think of, she sold it. I ended up dropping some stacks to get Big Ma a set of Vuitton luggage.

Whatever the case, no matter how much I tried, she still refused to give me her number. After my visit that day, I had decided to take her as a loss. Evidently, she was interested though, because I had merely mentioned that I had a store of my own and here she was. We started to walk my aisles.

"So what brings you to my city," I asked.

"I didn't know that this was your city."

"Ask around," I retorted confidently. "They call me Rah these days. I dropped the 'Heem in grade school."

She nodded and told me that she would keep that in mind and picked up a pair of True Religion jeans. I had the exact same pair on at the time. She checked the size and kept walking. She ended up grabbing a catalog off the top of a display and asked what it was for.

"That's a catalog of more items that True Religion has to offer. If you see something you like, I can have it delivered in 24 hours," I alerted.

She nodded; said that my idea was original and crafty. She asked if she could borrow my idea for her store. We walked over to the counter and I rang up her items. She asked what happened to her money being counterfeit around me. I handed her a receipt, grabbed her hand and started to escort her out of the building.

"Your money is counterfeit as long as you're spending it on yourself. It spends when you're purchasing shit for another nigga though."

She kept her mouth closed until we made it to the parking lot. Once I put her in my Escalade, she started to protest. I ignored her. There was no hostility in her voice. I crank up and headed for the Lexington Market. I had a taste for some fried ice cream. On the drive over, she glanced through my CD case. Finally, she asked what my girlfriend's name was. I gave her a curious look.

Fresh

"Heather Headley, Mary J, Maxwell, Jaheim…Either you got a sensitive side or your girl drives this truck," she analyzed.

I grinned to myself. She had a man herself so I didn't have a reason to stunt. I pulled down my sun visor and pointed at a picture of me and Diamond. She crawled over my lap to get a look.

"She's cute," she admitted.

"What time is your curfew," I asked as we pulled up to the market.

She replied that she had two hours to chill. We exited the whip and went to get some ice cream. Back in the truck, she asked me did I have any weed. I chirped Moneybags.

"That nigga diesel out there," I asked in code.

He told me that diesel was on deck and urged me to come through because he had something that he wanted to discuss with me. I gave Nika a look to see if all of this was okay with her. She hunched her shoulder as a response. Twenty minutes later, Moneybags hopped in the truck and passed some weed over the seat. He told me to circle the block real quick.

"Shit has been slow as fuck today. I'm nowhere near the quota," he complained.

I was shocked. Today is Thursday. Thursdays are almost better than Fridays in the hood. Before I could respond, we came up on Brice

Street. Traffic was everywhere. Shop was definitely open around this way. Only problem was I didn't have a shop on this corner. Before I could speak, Moneybags did.

"My mom came through and told me that some out of towners were around here selling some blue pills."

It was dark outside so I couldn't see specific faces. I did notice that the shops were operating out of T.O.'s properties. Nika lit up and passed me the blunt.

"So you say these are some out of towners," I asked just to be sure.

"I came around here to inspect personally. I've never laid eyes on none of these lames. But check this, they had the nerve to screw face me when I came through. It took everything in me not to recruit the boys and come back."

I asked him what his mom thought of the product. From the look of the fiends on deck, I could tell that they were pumping some raw shit. His answer baffled me.

"That's the thing Rah. My mom was like the dope is the same thing as we are pumping. The only difference is that it's labeled different and the pills are bigger." He took the blunt that I offered.

I stayed quiet, deep in my thoughts as I circled the block again. It was obvious that T.O. was trying to compete with me. I just couldn't figure which angle he was coming from. Yo owned most of the real estate in the neighborhood. If he wanted the hood to himself, his first move should've been to evict me.

"I'm saying though, the boys are all hyped and ready to move. I was just waiting on your call before making such a move. I mean, do we give them a fair warning to pack up and move or do we go in with guns blazing," he asked.

I circled the block once more. This was the third time and as expected, I was spotted by one of the lookouts. Unlike us, they used regular hustlers as spot men. That let me know that they had to be deep and organized. Like Moneybags, I had never seen any of them a day in my life. When I pulled back in front of our spot, it looked like a ghost town. This pissed me off.

"Yo, I'm gonna need to think for a minute. I'll need you to keep the boys in line until tomorrow. I should have my decision on how to handle this then." I gave him some dap before he exited.

After he got out, I circled the block one more time. T.O. was definitely on to something. Two could play games though. Since he wanted to act out, I'm ready to see his face when he comes to re-up and I tell him it's nothing. As far as the clowns he had set up shop with, they were gonna definitely get dealt with. I can't see myself compromising my hustle for anybody. I just couldn't give that order tonight, especially in front of Nika. I didn't know shorty enough for her to hear me conspire to murder anybody.

When we pulled back up at the mall, she directed me to park next to a candy apple red Aston Martin. Shorty was stunting harder than me. Before she made a move to exit the car, she placed her hand on my leg seductively.

"So you're the boss huh," she asked.

* * * * *

(Prince)

The sun wasn't even up as I trailed the Senator's Lincoln at a respectable distance. In my rearview, I saw no cars. I knew our destination though. We were headed to the Eco River to do a little fly fishing. It was Senator's every Saturday morning routine. The only difference with this Saturday is that it was gonna be his last.

Somehow, my pops convinced me that killing the Senator was a must. Because of the nature of the business, it was essential that I handle the job myself. With that understood, I recruited Twin as soon as I got home to fly to Atlanta and put in some prep work.

Princess' job in Georgia was to disguise herself and hire a private investigator to get any and everything they could find on the Senator. I sent her way down south to complete this task because I didn't want to leave a trail for the Feds. No info was given to the investigator. We paid generously, and in cash.

The profile delivered to me two weeks later was short and simple. The Senator is a widowed 62 year-old. He has one son, who is an assistant prosecutor in Houston. The Senator still occupies the family's ranch in Dallas, where he lives quietly. No woman has replaced his wife, yet he did have a girlfriend he fancied to escort him to political events and host his annual fourth of July bash.

Basically, he lived a quiet lifestyle. He had served in the Army for eighteen years before retiring honorably. His service in the senate has been impeccable. For the last thirteen years, he's circled the globe twice on the tax payers' money, chaired powerful committees, dined with three different Presidents and even had once run a Mafia Boss out of Dallas.

I arrived here in Dallas two weeks ago. With me, I had three different driver's licenses in assumed names. Three different rental cars and two separate hotel rooms were needed also. My weapon of choice was a Remington 30/30 deer rifle that I had stolen out of the window of a Chevy truck in a rodeo parking lot.

Even though the Senator's daily movements were documented in his file, I still trailed him to make sure. He never let me down either. Every morning, he ate breakfast at the same diner. While reading the newspaper, he consumes a breakfast of toast, grits, bacon and eggs. He'd drink two cups of coffee, socialize with the patrons and promptly leave the waitress five bucks.

He would arrive at his office no later than ten and always left at six. In between, he never left the office unless duty called. His routine was meticulous and boring. The way he acted, I thought the nigga knew someone was after his ass.

At home, he cooked his own meals. His lady friend usually joined him on Thursday nights and they would dine out. Afterwards, they would retire back to his place to play Gin Rummy.

After watching his routine for two weeks, I came to the conclusion that his fishing trips would be the perfect opportunity. The river was isolated, peaceful and quiet. The best part was that woods surrounded the river and they were used for hunting. Though I hadn't encountered any hunters, I often heard gunfire in the distance and saw signs advertising the season. With some luck, his murder would somehow look like a hunting accident.

When he made his usual turn to park, I kept straight to find my place. Yesterday, I had driven out this way to practice my escape route. To my surprise, now that the day was upon me, I wasn't even nervous.

Fresh

I found my hiding place along the river with ease. The sun hadn't fully risen yet, but I could see my victim heading out into the water perfectly. As I waited, I let my mind drift off to Baltimore.

The nigga Rah had the dope game in a stranglehold. We were pulling in so much money that I was trying to figure out a way to convince my pops to stay in the game when he came home.

As for my business, with mom's help, we had successfully lured the head foreman from a prominent firm in the city. With his expertise, we hired the best architects, pipe layers, and electricians that money can buy. Even though we hadn't landed any big contracts yet, I was learning the business and getting shit set up.

As for my relationship with Pia, it was time to see if we can stand the test of time. I knew that she suspected me of cheating from this trip alone. We argue every time I call home because I wouldn't tell her where I was and what I was doing. She naturally suspected me of being with some female.

Quita was back in the saddle and ready to ride for a nigga. After the big argument, I simply sent her roses, bought her a dress and fucked the shit out of her. She promptly fell back in line. The secret to short was attention.

Some movement in the water got my attention. The sun was coming up. The Senator was knee deep in the water with his back turned away from me. I raised my rifle to aim. Before I pulled the trigger, I said a quick prayer and asked God to forgive me.

* * * * *

(Princess)

Biggie Smalls said a mouth full when he made the term 'Mo Money, Mo Problems' popular. I was getting a taste of his motto firsthand. It all started last week when I received a citation from the ATF for selling liquor to a minor. The District allows two citations before it takes steps to shut an institution down. I had received my first already.

The whole incident was an open and shut case of entrapment. Of course, I ran straight to my mother with hopes that she would sue the government. It has to be some law against the government sending minors in an establishment to buy liquor. To my surprise, my mother informed me that what happened was completely legal. It wasn't shit that I could do but kick out for the fine and tighten up on my bartenders.

If that problem wasn't enough, I had been sitting at the club since 6:00 p.m. this evening waiting on a damn liquor truck to come stock my club. It's now a quarter after eight. Of course I had made numerous calls to the company, but couldn't seem to get through. I was scheduled to open in two hours and didn't have any fucking liquor.

Fresh

My manager Oz was supposed to handle these types of situations, but he had called in with a family emergency. The coincidence is that we had a problem with the cleaning service a couple of weeks ago and he had also called in about that.

My phone rang in my hand. The nigga Hood was in town at the moment waiting on me. He was trying to re-up and I hadn't had time to make the trip to Jessup. To make matters worse, my period had just snuck up on me and I wasn't gonna be able to get tightened up. I answered the phone sweetly anyway.

"My fault, Pa, but these people still haven't delivered my shit," I informed.

He asked me what time the club opened and wanted to know what I planned to do if the liquor didn't show up. I made my decision then to just call the liquor store, order up some goods and go pick up the liquor myself. Hood told me that he thought that was a good idea and not to worry about him. As soon as I hung up, I made the call.

I hung up quite proud of myself. No matter what hurdle that jumped in my way, I made due. I was starting to think that Oz was replaceable. After calling two of my bouncers to meet me at the package store, I made my exit. In the parking lot next to my Lexus, I spotted a Navigator with two goons standing beside it.

Both were dressed casually and big enough to play front line for the Ravens. I knew that they were muscle instantly. Instead of showing that I was intimidated, I politely smiled and informed them that the club didn't open for two hours.

The biggest one reminded me of Mr. T., complete with Mohawk and gold chains. The other one reminded me of the wrestler, Rock. Mr. T. opened the rear door.

"Mr. Ivan Harper requests a meeting with you. If you'll come with us, we will return you back here shortly."

Now I knew why they looked so familiar. They were bouncers at Love Nightclub and worked for its owner. Old boy Ivan was a big fan of mines. He wanted the pussy so bad and had tricked off plenty in my Love days trying to get it. He almost got lucky one night but after feeling him up, I decided he wasn't tall enough to ride this ride. Whatever the case, something told me that this wasn't a social call.

"Sorry fellas, but you'll have to tell your boss that I can't make it this time."

The Rock discreetly brandished a gun and stopped me in mid-sentence. He told me that Ivan only wanted fifteen minutes of my time and advised me to step into the truck. I decided to take his advice and got in the vehicle.

Fresh

Not once did I think of my club's liquor situation on the drive over. My mind was on Ivan and the audacity of him sending goons to kidnap me. And what was he trying to meet with me about anyway. Something told me that it was about the defection of his manager. Whatever the case, the truck pulled up to Love some twenty minutes later, and I marched inside to give him a piece of my mind. He was in his office doing some paperwork when I barged inside.

"I don't know who in the hell you think that you're dealing with, but you obviously got me fucked up," I snapped at his ass to get his attention.

His goons shut the door to give us some privacy. Ivan gave me that stupid grin of his before getting up to offer me a drink. I declined, asked him what his problem was and told him that I was in a rush. He nodded, poured himself a shot and swallowed quickly.

"This is some good shit. You sure you don't want a shot…" He stopped short and smiled. "Oh, I forgot, you probably have a whole club stocked full of this shit."

It was at that moment that I knew he knew about my liquor problem and probably had a hand in it. The only problem was how did he pull it off? I mean, I know yo had clout being that he's been in the business so long, but shutting down my liquor supply was just short of major. I guess from the look on my face, he could tell that I was trying to figure him out. Before I could comment, he spoke up.

"Listen beautiful, I'm just gonna give it to you straight. You're a big girl after all. Hell, anyone who can open up a nice club like you've done, steal my clientele and my manager, I figure can handle a little bad news."

I wanted to tell him that he could have his manager back and as for his clientele, I never put a gun to anyone's head and told them to attend my club. Instead, I stayed quiet.

"Bottom line is that partners invested in this club with me; some very powerful partners that are not too happy with you. They seem to think that you are the reason for the decline in our business…"

I cut him off and told him that I had nothing to do with the decline in his business. I informed him that I could point him in the direction of my PR firm; maybe they could come up with a better business plan to attract some of their customers back. With that said, I headed for the door.

"Quit being so bull headed and listen Princess. You may find what I have to say beneficial to you," he shouted and got my attention.

"First of all, who the fuck is this mysterious partner of yours," I demanded.

"Who he is, is not important and shall remain a secret. I will tell you that he was powerful enough to shut down your liquor supply with just a nod. And not only that, but that little cleaning problem you had two weeks ago, was his work also."

He had my attention then. Whoever yow a, he was sabotaging shit and it was no doubt in my mind that he could do worse. Furthermore, he had also just let me know that Oz was going to the unemployment line as soon as I left this office. His calling in wasn't such a coincidence after all. Seeing that he had my attention, he continued.

"As I was saying, my partners are not too happy with what you have going on. However, they respect the hustle. Instead of calling in some favors to have you shut down, my partners and I are willing to…"

I wasn't listening any further. My mind was made up. Obviously, they didn't know who they were fucking with. One phone call to Rah and he could have this whole club blown the fuck up.

* * * * *

(Gloria)

"I think that's poor judgment for an elder member to make. Next, all the children at the church will be using the restroom to do their hair," Big Ma complained.

We were in her kitchen. She was busy fixing me a sandwich so I could get back to work. I was on my laptop ordering birthday presents for my kids from their father. Sticking to his tradition, King was getting them matching gifts. Instead of the usual his and hers watches, he was stepping his game up this year. He was purchasing two Bentley continental G.T.'s. I was online now with a dealership practically building the cars from scratch.

For Prince, I chose the solid black car with black rims. He was so picky about his shit, I decided to leave his plain and let him hook it up. As for Princess, I know my daughter's taste. Shorty wanted to shine and I had the perfect idea. For her, I chose a hard top convertible joint. I got her name stitched in the head rest, floor mats, and dash. To really make her stand out, I ordered her shit painted Barbie pink with black rims. She was gonna love it.

The doorbell rang and got Big Ma's attention. Upstairs I could hear footsteps. My evil twin was up there on the prowl. I hadn't seen her in months. Even though I hated the bitch, a part of me wanted to see her face just to make sure she was alive and kicking. I got up to go see her.

Our beef went back over twenty years; the real beef that is. We hadn't really gotten along since junior high. The beef back then was just us being catty. We had been damn near inseparable since coming out of Big Ma's coochie. We were exact identical twins. The only way to tell us apart was the birth mark that she carried on her left ear. Big

Fresh

Ma dressed us alike until high school. Everything I had, she also had. We shared bedrooms, even though the house had three rooms. Every boy I liked wanted her, and vice versa. Basically, we were just tired of each other and were ready to find our own identities.

Our looks were where the similarities ended. We were as different as night and day in every aspect of life. In school, I excelled and shot for the stars, while Toria settled for average. When we got old enough to work, I got a job while she opted to run the streets. I preferred the library and a book while she chose the club and a blunt. I met King in the ninth grade and settled down, while she chose to bed hop.

King and I's relationship brought a lot of jealousy into the picture. Old girl was envious that I had old boy wrapped around my finger. She hated the fact that I had house trained a known dog. And the way he spoiled me didn't help either. The tension over my relationship in Big Ma's house caused me to move out in my junior year.

Sure we had our catty beefs, but she was still my sister. At times, we could get along. We still shared an unnatural bond because of the twin thing. I welcomed her into my house with open arms. That's where the big fall out occurred. Being that King had bread, of course he kept me dipped in nothing but the finest. Little shit started to get missing and when they turned up at Big Ma's shorty had the nerve to get an attitude with me over my shit. That was all material shit and I could deal with that. Hell, we had shared everything our whole life anyway. However, I had to draw a line when the bitch tried to steal my man.

The first incident occurred on a return trip from New York after attending an Eric B and Rakim concert. King had turned her on to his right hand man, a dude named Tyrell. Anyway, Tyrell was there in the limo with us but wasn't feeling to well. I was stretched out across King's lap trying to deal with a headache myself. Toria was drunk and still in the mood to party. I ignored her until she tried to pull some 'New Jack City' shit on me. The bitch got bold and told King that he deserved better than me; said that I was ungrateful and should be on my knees at the moment sucking his dick to show gratitude for all that he had done for me; even offered to bless him herself. I didn't let her go any further before I was all up in her shit. I got that ass real good in that backseat too. I got her again once the driver pulled over on I-95. And to make sure that she never tried a stunt like that again, I got her again the next day too.

Of course Big Ma got on her about not only that incident, but the way shorty was living life period. We already hated to be compared to each other so you can imagine how she took it when Big

Ma compared us that day. Shorty literally ran away. She quit school, found an old ass boyfriend to live with and got into the whole drug scene. We didn't see her for over three months. Her disappearance, the drug rumors and the mean streets of Baltimore had me worried. I went out personally to look for her, ready to apologize and squash the beef. I found her in East B-more looking bad and pregnant. The fucked up part was that the dude she was living with wasn't the baby's father.

Our biggest fallout, which led to the reason we barely speak today occurred about six months later when I got the call while at work from King informing me that I needed to come home. When I got there, he told me that she had let herself into our apartment with a key that she had possibly stolen off my keychain. Then she promptly got naked, and wiggled her pregnant ass in the bed with my man. He said that she claimed to be in love with him and begged him to let her make him feel good. He resisted and she stormed out of the house.

I went to Big Ma's to confront the dizzy bitch but was informed that I had just missed her. I started to chase after her but a comment that Big Ma caused me to stop. She had stated that Toria had entered the house, went to the basement and left straight out with a duffle bag. I immediately rushed to the basement to check for my shit. On the low, I had been holding some cash for King. When I made it to the basement, I immediately knew that the jealous bitch had got me. The old chest that I kept the money in was wide open and empty.

Anyway, I passed Big Ma while on the way upstairs to say hello. Big Ma asked me to grab her purse while I was upstairs. How about when I made it to her room, I saw that Toria had beaten me to her purse. The junkie bitch had stooped so stealing from our own mother. I shot straight to her ass too.

* * * * *

(Prince)

'My President is black/ My Lambo is blue/ and I'll be got damn if my rims ain't too...' I mumbled out loud to the lyrics of Young Jeezy as I made my way off the plane. I had ended up staying in Texas a couple more days after hearing the news about the Senator. For some reason, a nigga got paranoid and thought the airports were hot.

With all that behind me now, I spotted mom dukes near the baggage claim dressed in a Burberry trench coat and shades that I had copped for her on my trip to New York. I strolled over and planted a kiss on her cheek real quick. As usual, she was on the phone giving out orders to someone. It sounded as if she was telling Twin to get in touch with Rah and for them to meet us at the house.

"Is something wrong," I asked as I grabbed my bag off the turnstile.

"Nothing major," she replied as she looked me over. "I got a few details that I need to discuss with everyone."

She grabbed my flight information and saw that I was returning from Texas; stated that she thought I was in Atlanta for the last two weeks. I just grinned and continued out of the terminal. My being in Atlanta on business was the lie that I had told everyone except Twin. However, mom was too smart to believe my little fib and was searching for info.

I told her that I was hungry while behind the wheel of her Rover. I couldn't eat that bullshit that they served on the plane; shit tasted like rubber. I asked her if she had a specific appetite. I wanted seafood myself. She took off her shades and pointed to her eye.

"Seafood sounds good, but we'll have to call in that order. I can't go anywhere looking like this," she related.

I took one look at that eye and immediately thought the worst. I hit the interior lights to get a better view. Her right eye was swollen damn near shut. Anger rose out of me quicker than bile.

"I'm gonna kill that motherfucker. I should've got him when I caught his ass out there in NYC!" I slapped the dash in anger. "Where the fuck is he at? Call that nigga!"

She reached over to calm me and asked me who I was planning to kill; wanted to know what went on in NYC. I looked at her to see if she was trying to protect old boy. I saw that she was seriously clueless. Yo had been adamant about pursuing her since she broke it off with him. Thinking that he didn't take rejection well, I immediately assumed that he had done this to her. I reached for my phone, pulled up the pictures from NYC and showed them to her.

"I caught your boy in New York that time when I went shopping. They were in the same hotel that we stayed in. He didn't see me. I should have told you way back then..." I let my words trail off.

The evidence was right in her face. She skimmed through the pictures and the hurt was present. She had feelings for dude and it showed. Instead of tearing up, she merely grunted and passed me the phone back.

"Darius didn't do this to my eye. I caught Toria stealing out of Big Ma's purse and we got into it. She caught me with an elbow," she admitted while looking at her eye in the mirror.

I used the drive to her house to calm down. Princess and Rah were at the house when we arrived. After getting everyone a drink to sip on, we all gathered around the table. Ma took the floor; started telling us that we had to go to court in Cecil

Fresh

County next week for motions. Rah didn't know what motions were so I explained it to him.

"So what happens after motions," Rah asked.

"That depends on if there is even a case after motions," Ma explained. "So far, I've been able to convince one of the arresting officers to testify on our behalf."

This was new news even to me. I asked her how she pulled it off. She gave us the rundown on how she extorted old boy. After she finished, she did some calculations on a piece of paper and slid it in front of us.

"That is you guys' bill for my services. Twenty grand apiece for lawyer fees; the rest is what it cost me to grease up everybody's palms," she added.

The bill was well over a hundred grand. I could really care less about the amount of the bill as long as the case was going in our favor. Evidently, Rah could care less about the cost as well. He immediately grabbed my mother in a hug and started planting kisses on her face. Yo was so happy that he even offered to pay my half of the bill since it was his fault that I was involved. Once things were back calm, mom instructed us that she was about to teach us another little secret called 'tax write-offs.'

After she finished running that save money scheme down to us, she changed directions and asked us if we were familiar with a woman named Catherine Haynes. Rah recognized the name first.

"Isn't she a State's Attorney or something. I know she works somewhere in the courthouse," Rah questioned.

My mother nodded and smiled. She announced that Mrs. Haynes was in fact a State Attorney and also her sorority sister. Princess asked what she meant to us though.

"I received a call the other day from her asking for donations. It seems that my friend wants to be Governor of our fair state." She became quiet to let us digest that. "I think that she is perfect for the job too."

She went on to tell us what great qualities that her friend possessed and ended by asking if she could make a sizeable contribution on behalf of Phillips Incorporated. We all stared at each other, obviously not getting it. Rah asked the million dollar question this time.

"So if we make the donation, what is shorty gonna bring to the table?"

"With everything that we have going on as far as our legal situation, I think it would be good to have a friend like her on our team. Her influence could work wonders for our organization."

Fresh

After she put it that way, we all agreed that a donation wouldn't hurt. With all that cleared up, she asked if there was anything else. Rah raised his hand.

"I got a little problem on my end that I would like to run by y'all." We all waited for him to finish. "I got some out of towners that have moved around the way. They set up shop. I'm thinking of sending my hit squad in…"

Chapter 10

(Princess)

My chore for today was to chauffeur Big Ma around town on her errands. It was while she was inside a local Rite Aid that I received the call I had been waiting on.

"Who this," I asked, but fully aware.

"It's Ivan! Damn, let me find out that you don't have my number programmed in that phone?"

I gave him a phony laugh and told him that I lost the other phone and didn't have any numbers saved in this one yet. I put on my sexy voice and commented that I was definitely gonna program his in now though. I could hear his smile over the phone when he replied.

"That's what's up Ma. But on another note, what's up with that other thing?"

I put on my puppy dog voice and explained that my mother owned half of the club with me and I didn't want to holler at her about old boy's proposition. He started to cut me off but I went ahead. I told him that shorty was a lawyer and not accustomed to the ways of the streets.

Fresh

"I'm only a middle man in all this but I can assure you that my people are not trying to hear that Princess," he answered.

"I feel you on that too, but I was thinking…" I paused for an extra affect. "I was thinking that maybe you could talk to your people and in return, you and I could work something out. You know; me and you."

He pondered my request; asked exactly what I had in mind. I smiled to myself. Just like that, he was on the hook and ready to be reeled in.

The same night Ivan had approached me with his little proposition, I had ran everything down to Hood. Of course, Hood didn't like the idea of anybody trying to lean on me. He went berserk. We ended up putting our heads together and came up with the perfect plan. The plot called for me to lure Ivan to my club to discuss things so Hood could make him see things our way. Nevertheless, Ivan fell right into my hands and agreed that we should meet this weekend. As soon as I hung up with him, I dialed Hood's number to tell him the good news.

* * * * *

(Raheem)

"So you're so it's only six niggas around there," I asked Moneybags.

190

"Yo, not only is Mario little ass on the inside, but their top nigga is named Thug. He's trying to fuck with the bitch Lil' Shell from out Cherry Hill. Little Stevie from off Pennsylvania got a baby by that bitch. We're on the inside."

I hit the blunt and shuffled through the stack of bills in front of me. Little Mario was a youngin from our hood; a little bad ass nigga who we used as an errand boy. Every hood has one. Anyway, Moneybags put his ass on to the competition. Just as he had somehow grown on us, he also worked his magic around the corner.

From Mario's report, it was six niggas around there. T.O. rented them two houses. One was the shop and the other was used to rest. They changed shifts twice a day; working in sets of three. Two worked the product while the other counted the profit. They closed up each night at midnight.

My phone rang and took me back to the present. My little man Mike poked his head in the door before I could answer it and announced that my girl had just pulled up out front. I grabbed the stack of bills in front of me and stood up.

"Go see Murder personally and tell him to get his squad ready. I want this shit handled…"

Anxious to make a name for his self, Moneybags quickly explained that he had two niggas ready to make the move. I cut him short though.

"We're using Murder's people for this Money. What I need you and your boys to do is just shut down shop as usual. Only difference is that you and all the boys gonna go to Strokers tonight and have a good time on me," I instructed as I tossed the money in my hand to him.

He looked at the money and nodded; said that he understood now.

"You want us to be at the club just in case the people come asking questions. It's the perfect alibi," he grinned.

I nodded for more reasons than one. The part about the alibi was on point but the main reason I wanted them at Strokers was because T.O. owned the club. With them on deck there, it would throw him off even more.

I ended up giving him specific orders on how I wanted the job done. Niggas was eating good around the corner. The streets were starting to whisper that I was soft for allowing it. I couldn't wait to strike.

Outside, the shop was energetic as usual. The boys had a dice game going while other niggas got their grind on. Diamond, her sister Da'sha and Da'sha's friend Mya were sitting in my Escalade directly in front of the trap. Shorty climbed her sexy ass out to greet me.

"It took you long enough," she scolded. "You know I hate sitting in front of these hot ass spots. Let me find out that you had a bitch up in there. I was two seconds from coming in there.

I pulled her in for a quick kiss. She reached for the Checkers bag that was in my hand and asked how much was inside. Her and her people were going Christmas shopping down in VA somewhere. They were gonna be gone all day, which was fine with me. Old girl Nika had hit me earlier asking if I wanted to ride with her for a little while. I hadn't seen shorty since that night at the store. I was actually anxious to lay eyes on her.

"That's like twenty three. Make sure you get Big Ma something she'll actually wear this time, Diamond. She's not into all that Gucci shit," I advised.

She replied that she was on point this year and made her exit. No sooner than she made it off the block, Nika called and asked where I wanted to meet. I told her that the Galleria was fine and rushed to my whip. I found her parked in her Aston Martin fifteen minutes later. She motioned for me to join her in her car. As soon as I was seated inside, she leaned over and planted a soft one on my lips. I took advantage of the situation and offered my tongue. She took it, and sucked real nice and slow. I found her rhythm but she pulled back.

"Wooo...I haven't been kissed like that in a while. Like how you work that tongue, boss man," she complimented.

"You should let me show you what else I can do with it," I responded with a wink.

She laughed and told me to buckle up before she ended up accepting my offer.

* * * * *

(T.O.)

"So basically what you're telling me is that your agency has had this Mr. Phillips under investigation for the last five months. He just had a case in Cecil County that was Nolle Prosequi last week. You've been unable to keep a tap on his phone because he disposes of them daily." My lawyer rifled through the paperwork in front of him and stared at the agents in disbelief. "Essentially, you guys have nothing against this man, yet want my client's help in trying to apprehend him?"

My eyes shifted from my lawyer, Randy Shroder, a hard-nosed defender who had been representing me and my best interest for over twenty years now, back to the agents. In all, it was three of them. I knew one personally. Agent Tom Mayes had arrested me back in the day and succeeded in turning me against my friend. He was now retired, but was at this meeting to make me feel uncomfortable.

The two others were still active DEA agents. The lead was a dyke Hispanic broad by the name of

Susan Cartagena. The other cat was named Mark Alberts. He stayed quiet and observed everything.

In a nut shell, you're right..." Agent Cartagena started before Randy cut her off.

"And the only link to my client and the suspect that you have is that you followed him to my client's auto shop on numerous occasions?"

Susan nodded but assured us that they had witnessed me and Rah having several whispered conversations during these meetings. Randy countered that it was on the record that the target had actually purchased a car from my dealership and threw out that we could've been merely talking about his warranty. Before she could answer, he also brought up that during these so called meetings, they had never witnessed anything suspicious passed between me and Rah. Tired of being cut off in mid-sentence, she merely nodded and smiled mischievously.

"So to sum up my conclusion, you don't have shit but an informer telling you myths, yet you're here asking us to help you build a case. And if my client refuses and I must add that as of now I will advise my client to refuse; however, if my client does refuse to assist and you somehow connect the two and are able to indict, you intend to prosecute to the fullest."

Susan waited until he was finished before agreeing that he was correct. She stated that this meeting was about a procedure the agency liked to call 'fair warning.' She went on to explain and pushed some papers in front of us. In a nut shell, the government wanted to offer me immunity early to help them out. I noticed that Randy didn't even look at the paperwork before sliding it back in her direction.

"I'm familiar with the procedure Ms. Cartagena. What concerns me is what exactly you would want my client to do in order to assist you. And if my client agrees to help and is not able to produce the evidence you all need, will he be exonerated or harassed further," Randy questioned.

Susan pushed the contract back over and explained all concerns would be answered after we read. The trick was that if I signed aboard, I would have to do it today for security purposes. They were scared that I would sign on and then try to alert Rah to the situation. What they didn't know was that I was ready and willing to join their team. A nigga got too much to lose to risk my freedom fucking with a street punk.

* * * * *

(Prince)

"Are you registered to vote next week," Quita asked as we sat in the food court of the Owing Mills mall.

"Wouldn't miss it for the world; I think it's gonna be the biggest turn out in voting history. Even Rah crazy ass registered this year," I let on.

She nodded and fed me a nacho and cheddar chip. She said that she was all for Obama and change. We chatted about politics for a few. It amazed me how ghetto shorty was on the outside, yet could get articulate as if she graduated from Yale. I always enjoyed our intimate conversations and the time we spent together. I glanced at the floor and the bags that we had accumulated. I asked her if she was finished spending my bread for one day. Then I told her to scratch that and added that she could spend all the bread she wanted as long as she didn't make me tag along any further. She held out her hand.

"In that case, I'll call you later."

I gave her some dap and we prepared to leave. We had spent the entire day doing some early shopping for the baby. The doctor said we were having a boy and I was excited. After getting that information, I insisted on going shopping for the nursery.

As soon as we got out into the regular mall traffic, it sounded like I heard my daughter Asia yell my name. Turning around to look was my first mistake. How Asia noticed me from the back and ten feet away, I have no idea. There she was in all her glory and of course Pia was with her. Our eyes met for a brief second before she handed Asia over to her mother and came my way.

Pia knew about Quita's and my past. Back in the day when we first hooked up, I was recovering from my breakup with Quita. They had history of their own. When Quita found out I was moving on, but also with a half black, half Korean chick, she tried to bully shorty. Little Ms. Pia had some spunk and wasn't going for it. They ended up getting a few rounds in back then. I was determined not to let round two happen today.

"Go ahead out to the car. I'll handle this and be right out," I said to Quita as I passed her my keys.

She rolled her eyes, gave me a stubborn look, but accepted the keys anyway. Pia waited until she disappeared before speaking. Her first question was if I was back fucking with shorty.

"Nah, it ain't even like that," I explained with a straight face. "I was out here getting some Jordan's and happened to bump into her. She needed a ride and I told her yeah."

Her eyes went to the bags in my hand. I wanted to slap myself immediately. There wasn't a sneaker bag in sight. She reached for a bag and inspected it.

"This is her stuff…" I began.

"Stop lying," she yelled so loud that Asia immediately started crying. "You are messing with that girl again and I know it so please stop lying."

I may be a lot of things but a chump I'm not. There was no way I was gonna admit no shit like that in the middle of the mall, especially in front of my daughter and the whole world. I reached to pull her close and mumbled something about discussing it later. She stepped out of my grasp, yelled something in Korean and then hit me with the English translation.

"You are messing with her and she's pregnant. I'm done with your trifling ass!"

* * * * *

(Raheem)

When Nika left Baltimore, back in the day, her and her people relocated to Philly. That was where we were now. After chilling with her mom and eating a healthy meal, she was giving me the tour of the streets of 'Killadelphia.'

"Where we at now," I asked inspecting my surroundings.

She mentioned that we were in North Philly. She said that she was looking for someone. The city reminded me of home actually; everything from the abandoned row houses to the junkies nodding off on every corner. The biggest difference I noticed was that there were a lot of Muslims.

Fresh

"There that bitch go right there," Nika noticed suddenly before pulling over in front of a bodega.

Street niggas were out in full blast. Nika yelled out to a female who was profiling on the hood of a Porsche. Shorty looked up and tilted her D&G shades to get a better view. The hustlers admired the whip. Shorty noticed Nika and immediately came out way.

"No you didn't Biotch; a fucking Aston Martin Vanquish," shorty, who I later found out was named Foxy, squealed.

Nika stepped out the car to give her a hug. A curly head big nigga wearing a triple fat Coogi goose grabbed her in a bear hug and slung her around. I stepped out the car then to make my presence known. The nigga didn't even look my way.

"Damn, Ma, you finally made it home to holler at the common folk." He scolded her before glancing at me. "And you know better than to be making all of that commotion out here. I got to work baby!"

She apologized and then introduced me. The big dude name was Big Mo. He shook my hand warmly, introduced me to a couple of his boys and told me that I was good people if I was fucking with Nika. I gave them some time to catch up as I enjoyed the dice game that they were putting on. A thousand dollars poorer and an hour later, Nika stepped out the car.

"Baby, its Foxy's birthday tomorrow, and she's throwing a party tonight. I want to go so bad, but I'll understand if you need to get back," she cooed.

"She'll understand, but I won't. If you need to get home, I'll have one of my people drive you, but my girl staying tonight," Foxy demanded.

I held my hand up and told shorty to calm down. I didn't really feel like staying up this way, but wasn't about to miss the opportunity of hitting Nika either. I told her that I was with it but reminded her that we didn't have anything to wear. That was the least of our worries. We headed straight to the mall. On the drive there, I made my pitch.

"So which hotel are we staying at?"

She gave me a look so I decided to clean it up. I told her that I was gonna need somewhere to change and shower up. She put her hand on my thigh and rubbed.

"A room won't be necessary tonight. We'll freshen up at my mom's crib and you can sleep in my bed tonight."

She didn't get any complaints from me. At the mall, we both put in needed calls to our spouses. Diamond didn't give me any problem at all, but Nika was going through it. She finally ended her call by telling yo that she was coming home. When she hung up, I asked if we had a change of plans. She popped her lips.

"Fuck that nigga. His ass all the way in Miami with his baby's mother and think he can control shit this way. I wish I would go home!"

We ended up putting it down at the mall. I made shorty model a couple of outfits for me to inspect. She was killing everything and guaranteed that nothing would touch her that night. As we were leaving Nordstrom's, I noticed a familiar face. It was Prince's connection. Evidently, he noticed me too because he couldn't take his eyes off of me. I steered Nika in his direction.

"Luis," I asked.

"Prince Familia," he responded.

I reminded him of my name and we shook hands. He wanted to know what I was doing in Philly. I ran down some excuse and he nodded. He had a big dude with him that seemed agitated. He started to talk to him rapidly in Spanish. The big dude seemed to lighten up once Luis told him who I was.

"I spoke to your cousin the other day. I'm supposed to be making a trip down that way this weekend," Luis offered.

Hearing that was good news. I still didn't know the full details of the operation. I didn't know exactly how many bricks these cats were flooding the city with. What I did know was that the shit was moving like hot cakes, the fiends were happy and plenty of money was being made.

"That's what's up. Come on through. Business is good around the way."

His brother spoke to him again. They talked for a second in Spanish. When he turned back to me, his request was surprising.

"Listen, I hope I'm not overstepping my boundaries. The boy Prince told me that you were the HNIC down that way. My brother here respects business and the quality of your product, but the prices are a little too steep; especially with the amount of shit we are getting from you guys. It's not a drought anymore however my brother wants to keep…"

I wasn't listening anymore. If what I was hearing was correct, this dude was telling me that he was copping from us. That meant that they weren't the plug and that we were; not we, but Prince. I wracked my brain back to the day Prince first came to me about the work and could specifically remember him saying that the amigos were the plug. Whatever the case, something wasn't right and it was evident that Prince was lying to me.

* * * * *

(T.O.)

Fresh

Shit was official. As of a few hours ago, I became an official informant for the United States government. The condition of the contract was for me to get Rah to my shop to discuss a drug transaction. It was a one shot deal so I took it. Shroder put in some specific conditions to protect me and I made a good faith call right in front of the agents. Unfortunately, Rah didn't pick up.

After they let me go, I retreated back here to my penthouse; had to get on my safe phone and make some calls to the Cayman Islands. The visits from them boys today scared the shit out of me. Of course they knew about all the legal shit, such as the partnership in Diane's firm, the eight dealerships, the club and the Subway franchise. That didn't mean that they weren't digging into my other affairs. So to be on the safe side, I was busy moving money into off shore accounts when the doorbell rang.

Diamond came in carrying groceries along with her Gucci book bag. After planting a soft one on my lips, she dropped her bags off in the kitchen and headed for the bedroom. I finished my business and joined her. She was on the toilet. I smiled because shorty even looked good relieving herself.

"You plan cooking for me tonight," I asked.

She nodded and asked if I liked ox tails. She said that she thought it was time for her to show me her kitchen skills. She washed her hands then went to her Gucci bag.

"I picked you up something today while I was out shopping," she alerted.

I was in shock once she produced two jewelry boxes from her bag. A nigga not used to a broad buying me anything. This one was a keeper even though she was stepping out on old boy. I opened the box. Inside was a set of platinum cuff links with a diamond set in the middle. The second box revealed a matching tie clip. I pulled her in close for a kiss.

"I thought that you would like it considering that you got your grown and sexy thing going on," she teased.

Everything about shorty was turning me on. She tried to pull away but I wouldn't let her. I grabbed that ass and gave it a squeeze.

"Hold up playboy. That's my spot!"

"And that's what I know," I answered as I scooped her into the air.

Fresh

Chapter 10

(Prince)

I woke up to a pounding on the door. Someone was knocking like the police. I yelled a few curse words to no avail. Finally, I got up to see what the racket was about. It was Pia.

"Open the door you cheating motherfucker. I know that you're in there," she screamed.

Due to the fallout, I was crashing at Princess' crib. How she made it pass the doorman, I have no idea. Just as I reached for the top lock, she produced a bulldog .357 Magnum and used the butt to bang on the door.

"If I tell you to open this door one more time…"

I told her to get a hold of herself and put that fucking gun away. She wasn't hearing me though; said she would only put the gun away after she received some answers. She told me that I had until the count of three to open up or she was gonna proceed to act a fool.

"One…Two…"

I could hear my neighbor open her door and gasp at the sight in front of her. I peeped out the hole and saw her take a step back and aim.

"Alright…Alright… Just tell me what you want to know and I'll answer it," I complied.

She seemed to contemplate this for a second before finally asking was the baby shorty was carrying mines. I didn't hesitate figuring that the truth would make her angrier so I responded that the baby wasn't mines. Her response was…

"Wrong answer bitch; three…" She pulled the trigger.

"Aaah…" I yelled and fell off the couch. A quick glance around the room revealed that I was indeed at Princess' place. The ashtray in front of me had like four half smoked blunts in it. The empty bottle of Patron explained the splitting headache I had. The knocking at the door let me know that someone was really knocking and extremely mad. My dream came back to me in a flash. Princess stumbled out of her room, closing her robe.

"Alright, I'm coming! Who the fuck is it!"

Quita waltzed in complaining that she had been knocking for a little minute. She stopped in her tracks once she saw me. Yesterday's events flooded my memory. After the incident in the mall, I dropped her ass off and rushed to D.C. Pia was there along with her father, brother, and mother. They were busy packing my shit up. Her father explained that she didn't want to talk at the moment. He said that I should give her a few days before I tried to reconcile. Yo was real respectful, plus Gloria raised me right so I didn't act up. Instead, I just threw all of my shit into the Magnum and retreated to B-more.

I got to B-more and tried calling Pia a few times. She wasn't fucking with me though. Quita was leaving messages on my shit like crazy. The first few were for me to call her. She switched gears after a few and called me some names; yelled that she never put a gun to my head to fuck her and then reminded me that it was my idea to go shopping anyway. She calmed down after she spoke her mind and apologized. Instead of calling her, I dialed Pia's number and got through.

"I hope that you enjoy your new baby because you won't get a chance to see the one that I'm carrying in my stomach, you cheating motherfucker," she yelled before hanging up.

It was that message, the thought of Pia being pregnant and aborting that drove me to the bottle. The bottle put me in that drunken sleep which led to me waking up to this.

Quita stood in front of me with her hands on her hips. In her eyes, I saw plenty of mixed emotions. Princess stood beside her with a look of astonishment on her face. She didn't know what the situation was about. This morning was the first time I had saw her in days. I was glad she was there now though.

Fresh

"I'm going back to bed," Princess announced and pointed a warning finger at me. "Make sure that you clean up behind yourself. Your ass don't have a maid."

She headed for her room. I headed for the restroom. When I came out, Quita was busy cleaning up. I pointed the remote at the TV and turned on the news.

"You know that was some fowl shit that you pulled yesterday, right," she accused.

I wasn't listening to her. The reporter on the news had my attention. She was broadcasting live from West Baltimore on the scene of what she described as a home invasion/ multiple homicides. According to her, eight unidentified men were found in a row house; tied, gagged and shot execution style. She reported that no suspects were being sought but that it was still early in the investigation.

* * * * *

(Raheem)

The constant ringing of a phone woke me out of my slumber. I glanced around at my surroundings. Last night came back in a blur. We hit the club for Foxy's party and had a ball. Old girl was really a force to be reckoned with in Philly. There was nothing but money in the building. Not only did Petey and Freeway come through, but

Beanie Siegel and Gillie the kid also showed love. Shorty copped the bar and must've lain out like three pounds of diesel. They even had baby bottles of syrup and free X-pills for the partygoers.

Nika surprised me and took a couple of sips off the bottle herself. When she offered the bottle to me, I declined, but gladly accepted a few pills. Whatever the case, we got tore up from the floor up; ended up back here at her mom's crib in the basement which was set up for Nika's visits.

Shorty stripped down to her thong and climbed instantly into the bed when we got in. The pill was playing tricks with my stomach. After a shit and a shower, I slipped into the bed only to find her snoring. I ended up falling out with a hard dick. And that's exactly how the phone woke me up too.

I nudged Nika to get her attention. She snuggled closer; told me that her mother would answer it. A second later, a light came from upstairs and her mother yelled that the phone was for her. Instead of grabbing the receiver, she put on the intercom.

"Hello," she mumbled. Her boyfriend's voice came through loud and clear. He wanted to know why she wasn't at home like he told her to be. She muttered some lame shit about her family coming over and everybody getting drunk. He wasn't trying to hear it though.

"Quit lying Nika. Your ass is just determined to…"

She cut him off by yelling for her mother to pick up the phone. I could tell that they had done this before because her mother happily relayed the same tale that she had just spit to him. Nika took that moment while they were on the phone to reach back and massage my dick. I kissed her neck and tweaked her nipples until Mrs. Carter hung up.

"Happy," she asked with an attitude.

"Whatever, anyway, I need you to do something for me."

She sighed, showing frustration and then pulled me on top of her. While Ray was relaying his message to her, she was letting me get comfortable between those soft thighs. He wanted her to go pick up some package from a spot in D.C.

"What am I supposed to be picking up Ray? You know…"

"Don't worry about that. Just have your ass at the meet on time and get my shit," he said before the line clicked.

As soon as he hung up, I moved from her breast to her navel and even lower. Her pubic hairs were trimmed to perfection. Instead of removing her thong, I simply pushed them to the side and went for the clit.

"Oooh yeah, that's what I'm talking about."

Unlike most niggas, I'm quite at home with my head buried between some thighs; not just any thighs though. I got a sixth sense for sweet pussy. I'm like a radar detector. When I'm with a girl who deserves my tongue action, my whole mouth will get wet to alert me that she is worthy. This pussy was definitely signaling me. I decided to reach in my trick bag and used my thumb on the clit while my trigger finger went for the asshole. She liked that shit; had her legs shaking like she had the chills when she came.

"Shit boy...now that's what I'm talking about," she yelped while pushing my face away from her dripping pussy. I reached for her but she balled up in a fetal position. "Wait...I just need a minute or two."

I laughed out loud, quite pleased with myself. I got up and hit the restroom. I washed my mouth out in the sink and winked at myself in the mirror. I beat on my chest like the warrior that I knew I was then prepared to go finish her off.

She was bent over inside her mini fridge when I stepped back into the room. I sat on the bed and admired that heart shaped ass of hers. I noticed that she had 'Baby Ray's' tattooed on the small of her back. I got a little jealous. She approached the bed and handed me a bottle of O.J.

"You were right," she said as she sat beside me.

Fresh

"Right about what," I asked.

"Your tongue game, it's nice...haven't gotten any head like that in a long time. My pussy feels sooo good right about now," she said and rubbed herself for emphasis.

I swigged from the bottle, reached for the ashtray to retrieve the blunt from last night. Shorty headed for the restroom. I grabbed my phone to check my message. I had one from Moneybags letting me know that all was good in the hood. Nika entered the room, thongless and crawled up the bed like a panther stalking its prey. She took the blunt from me, pulled it and then told me to relax.

Using her tongue, she started with my face and worked her way down to my feet. When she made it back up to her prize, I was ready for whatever. She kissed the head slowly, ran her tongue along its length and then started to massage it with her hand.

"Grab that pillow; don't want you yelling and shit. My mom might get worried," she commanded with a wink before going down for a deep throat.

She wasn't a stranger to the wood. Baby Ray had trained her right. She had technique; knew how to relax her throat and take me to the back of that fucker. Her hands were in perfect sync with her mouth. She even understood that spit was the key to good head. She had me ready to cum in no time and didn't procrastinate about swallowing. She even kept going until I was ready for seconds. After using her mouth to put a condom on, she got onto all fours, put her face in the pillow and looked back at me.

"Get back there and work her out!"

She didn't have to tell me twice. I gave her my all. I went hard into the pussy because I knew that was what she wanted. I stroked her long and deep; then short and fast. She loved every minute of it; gave it back to me as good as she got it and used her pussy muscles like a champ. She ordered me to smack her ass; played with my balls to make me even harder, while sucking on her fingers like they were a dick. When she came, she jumped from one end of the bed to the other.

I wasn't through with that ass yet and chased her. My radar was up. I wanted to suck that pussy once more; told her to sit on my face. I put my finger back in her ass and she went crazy. She immediately bent forward and took me into her mouth. She got a good rhythm going before snatching the rubber off. She crawled around to give me her full attention. Then she went for my balls. I felt her going to the place between my nuts and my asshole. I started to run then. She gave chase.

She grew tired of the chase, rolled onto her back and spread her legs into a V-shape. Then she told me to come get it. I went for another rubber and proceeded to do as she asked.

* * * * *

(T.O.)

I showed up to the dealership sometime after noon whistling an Earth, Wind and Fire tune. My employees all gave me a curious glance. Even Ray Charles could see that I had gotten laid good last night.

Old girl Diamond did her thing. After the wonderful meal that she cooked, we took a long luxurious bath together. Afterwards, she pulled out some oils and treated me to a full body massage until I fell asleep. She woke me up with a blow job. Then, gave me the pussy raw for the first time; let me skeet all up in that kitty cat, then pulled out the KY and let me tap that ass, literally.

I hadn't been cared for and then sexed that good since the early stages of my marriage. Her actions only confirmed that she was a keeper. We stayed up late pillow talking. I think she was starting to catch feelings for me too. She got a little background info out of me. I even told her about my daughter that lived down south. She was shocked to learn that. I told her that it was privileged information and only a select few knew about her.

She spoke a little about Rah and hers relationship. She told me that he was out of town at the moment on business, but didn't let it slip exactly where he was. I came right out and asked her if she was happy with old boy. After a little hesitation, she admitted that she was. She explained that he was all that she really knew; said that me and yo were the only two men ever. She admitted that the thing with me had only supposed to be a onetime thing to get back at him for all of his past indiscretions, but somehow, she liked what I did to her. She said that I paid attention to her both mentally and physically and she needed that in her life.

Either the broad was telling the truth or she deserved an Oscar. For some reason, I believed every word that came out of her mouth. I decided right then that as soon as those people scooped up Rah's ass, I was gonna make it my business to scoop up his girl.

My assistant Kristen met me on the showroom floor. She stuck those D-cups out for me to inspect before handing me a sheet of paper. She informed me that a Raven's manager had just called about a Ferrari that I was supposed to order. She also reported that there was trouble at my Cadillac dealership that needed tending to. She finished with a wink and a view of those long legs.

As soon as I finished handling the necessary business, Bruh stuck his head into my office. He wanted to talk business so we headed for the Maybach. After I was comfortable in the back, he gave me the news about Thug and his crew. He talked like Rah had left him in a bad way. Yo was definitely trying to send a message. The question is was it me that he was sending the message to. Bruh was reading my mind, but asked the question out loud.

"I don't know what the nigga is up to. I'm pretty sure that Thug probably told them niggas that we invited them up here," I confessed while reaching for a Nestea from my fridge.

"Think I should put in a call to Bonnie," Bruh asked.

Don Corleone had Luca Brasi. The Jamaicans in the movie 'Belly' had Shy'Quita. I had Bonnie. Shorty was my secret weapon; a hired assassin. She was a thoroughbred bitch who could leave you bleeding in the streets or choking on untraceable poison. The best thing about shorty was that she was a master of disguise. Yo could play a dope fiend, an exotic dancer or a real estate agent. And she never missed her man either. I shook my head.

"Hold off on shorty. I think I'm gonna meet with yo face to face first just to get a feel on him," I let on.

* * * * *

(Princess)

After letting Quita in, I crawled into bed and snuggled up to my company. Quita showing up like that only confirmed my suspicion that something was up with her and Twin. When I found him drunk and dead to the world on my couch last night, I knew that all wasn't good in paradise. The vibe between him and Quita said that it was serious too. As nosey as I wanted to be, I was stuck between a rock and a hard place when it came to those two.

Nevertheless, Hood stirred when he felt my touch. He was in town to handle that situation with Ivan tonight. He moaned out loud at my touch and mumbled that he needed to pee. When he reentered the room, he stopped in his tracks.

"Tell me that isn't your loud ass girlfriend Quita out there," he asked.

I nodded him and reminded him that Prince was out there too. A paranoid expression came over his face as he went to check the lock on my bedroom door. He mumbled that he was already taking a risk with Prince being in the house. He said that he definitely didn't want Quita getting wind the here was here too.

"You need to calm your paranoid ass down. They are not thinking about you or me. Shit, they got some shit going on between them anyway. And I don't care how much you think Quita run her mouth, you should know that she wouldn't tell no one about you being in town."

Fresh

He gave me a look; probably wanted to argue his point but knew how I could get. I patted the bed beside me. After he sat, I crawled behind him and started to massage his shoulders. I told him that I understood his predicament but putting my brother out was out of the question. He nodded. I started to plant kisses on his neck and laid him down. The phone rang. I ignored it and concentrated on him. Right when I had him ready and relaxed, Twin knocked on the door and announced that my mother was on the phone.

* * * * *

(Raheem)

"My girl like you," Nika said.

We were about to hit the exit and enter the city. My mind was elsewhere. Prince was in my thoughts. I reached for my phone to text him.

"Did you hear what I said," Nika asked. I gave her a look. "I said that my girl Foxy like you. She may want to give you some pussy."

I let out a laugh. She grinned but never let her eyes leave the road. I knew that she was serious then. A flashback of them dancing last night came to me. They were a little touchy feely. Something was definitely up with those two. She looked over at me and winked; asked what I thought of that. If it was a trick question, I failed.

"I'm not scared of pussy. You should know that."

She hit me playfully and mumbled something about niggas not being shit. My phone vibrated and got my attention. It was Prince letting me know to stop by Princess' crib. Nika was pulling up beside my car by the time I finished replying. She nodded at the whip.

"Nice wheels you got there; is that a '07?"

I looked at my wheels before correcting that it was a 2008 model. I smacked her dashboard and told her that my shit had nothing on the amazing machine we were riding in. She looked at her watch real quick before leaning in for a kiss. This time it was her who offered her tongue. She moaned that she really enjoyed herself and wanted to know when I could get free again.

"I can come and go as I please," I answered with a pat to my chest. "If I recall, it's you who gets the wake up calls."

She laughed before getting serious. She said that her man would be back in town the next day and wanted to know if it was possible to repeat last night. I hesitated and she cut me off.

"No pressure, but check it. He goes back out of town this Tuesday. Foxy claimed that she wants to come down and hang out. I was thinking of taking her to your cousin's club."

Fresh

I nodded and told her that Tuesday was good. Princess was planning a birthday/ Presidential celebration for after the polls closed down. She had T-pain and Gucci Mane coming through.

We parted ways after another kiss. I hopped in the Beamer and headed for Federal Hill. Prince came straight out the building ready to talk. He gave me the rundown on his, Pia's and Quita's situation. I stayed quiet and listened. Two babies on the way and Pia threatening to abort hers; I knew of his and Quita's history. I also was aware of her wild side. Still, I knew that her heart truly belonged to my boy. Nevertheless, I thought that it was a bad idea for him to lose or leave Pia for Quita. Statistically, Pia was the best woman for him. He knew how I felt about the situation so there was no need for me to give him the third degree. He was looking for advice so I cranked up and drove him to the place I went to when Diamond got mad at me. He gave me a crazy look when I pulled up.

"Every kiss begins with Kay, bruh. Let's go in here and pick out something nice for both of them. Trust me, they'll both forgive you."

Prince really wanted forgiveness and pointed out a 3 ½ carat engagement ring for Pia and a matching set of bracelets for Quita. I teased that forgiveness didn't mean tying the knot, but he was adamant that it was what he needed to do to show is intent to be serious. We left the jewelry store and headed for the hood to cop some smoke. I decided to bring Philly up on the drive.

"I was in Philly yesterday at the mall and ran into your boy Luis," I mentioned casually.

He was busy texting on his phone and didn't look up. He did manage to ask what I was doing way in Philly at the mall. After I told him, he just nodded.

"Yo was with his brother. They asked me about lowering the prices for them."

I studied him for a reaction. He still didn't look up from his phone. Instead, he merely shrugged his shoulders, so I went more in depth.

"His brother was complaining; said something about how big he'd been copping from us and that it's only right that we drop the prices for him."

"Drop the prices my ass. Yo, I've been selling them wetbacks fifty joints at seventy five apiece. The going rate for the quality of our shit is ninety. You should have told that nigga to kiss your ass!" He got animated and swung his hands in the air. "Hell, your man cops the same amount if not more and he don't even get that price."

I held my hands in the air and told him that I was only the messenger. On the inside, I was boiling though. Not only had he lied to me about the plug, but he was also making money behind my back. I felt betrayed.

Fresh

"You gonna have to tell yo to go to hell yourself. I don't even have yo number. Shit, I didn't even know we were selling them any work. I thought they was the plug," I added with a sarcasm in my voice.

Prince gave me a look. After a moment he nodded and motioned for me to pull over. He looked me dead in the eyes as he spoke.

"You're right that I didn't tell you about the connection but I did that shit for good reasons. The niggas I'm dealing with are demanding secrecy and I'm gonna respect their wishes. On the other hand, we're eating real good, so I figured you could care less about who the plug was."

He had a point about respecting yo's wishes for secrecy. If I was in his predicament, I would probably keep my plug a secret too. Still, I had a good argument to get off of my chest.

"I can live with you keeping the plug to yourself. Still, I would think that you would have more faith in me to keep it a secret but..."

"Oh, there you go on some Boston George shit..." he started before I cut him off.

"Like I said, I can respect the secrecy. What I can't respect is the fact that you're holding out on me period. You've been making money on the side and all. I've been out here in the trenches and have split every dime I've made with you. Yet, here you go making damn near millions behind my back. What's that about," I asked.

He studied me for a minute before reaching for a decent blunt roach in the ashtray. After lighting up, he claimed that I was on some petty shit. He stated that if my argument was about money, then he would start splitting the take with me.

"My beef is about the money and the trust fam. Here I am out here getting a ghost rich and I don't even know the motherfucker. And to top it off, all that whining you did about staying low and under the radar, but I find out that you've been hustling too. Fuck that, we a team! You eat and I eat."

I pulled over on my block and looked around to find someone with some weed. Prince grabbed the door handle and got out. Before walking off, he motioned for me to roll down the window.

"Niggas kill me. I come through with the work and make us both young millionaires in six short months. You've been out here hustling for years and haven't seen this much money but yet you want to fuss..."

He stopped and took a deep breath. Yo was overheated. Before I could say anything, he stuck his head in the window.

"Check it cuzzo. We got something good going here. You want your cut off the Philly situation then I got you. But I want to run something by you since you think that you're the only one out here putting in work. A couple of weeks ago when I was out of town, I was busy putting in work for the connection. I had to go kill a motherfucker nigga. I'm risking my life to help you and the fucking plug get rich and I'm not complaining either. What you need to do is just chill the fuck out and count this money," he said before walking off.

I didn't even call after him. He needed to calm down. I needed to digest what he'd just told me. No way was the nigga lying. Before he told me that, I wouldn't have believed he could bust a grape in a fruit fight. A junkie knocked on my window and held up some cleaning supplies to get my attention. I nodded and prepared to go apologize to my cousin.

* * * * *

(T.O.)

After Bruh dropped me back at my shop, I jumped into my Porsche and made the trip to the D.C. Federal building. The fibbies wanted me to try the phone call for them again. The meeting was held in D.C. for security reasons.

Shroder met me in the garage so we could go over a couple of things in the elevator. We were met in the conference room by Susan and Mark from yesterday. After pleasantries, we got down to business. I made the call on my cell. Rah didn't pick up until the fifth ring and when he did, he sounded aggravated.

"Damn nephew, is this a good time," I asked him.

"Who this?"

"Who else calls you nephew? Let me find out you don't know my voice after I've damn near raised you," I said and gave a wink to the fibbies.

He apologized. I could tell he was checking his caller ID. He said that he didn't recognize my voice or the number that I was calling from. The number was unfamiliar because I usually used Bruh's phone to call him. He commented that didn't many people have the number I had just called then casually asked how I got the number. I ignored his question and asked where he'd been hiding lately.

"I've been busy working, Unc. You know I got the store in the mall now. I've been busy selling clothes man."

I told him that I had heard somewhere that he was selling clothes these days. Before I could go any further, he cut me off and announced that he had an important call on the other line that he needed to answer. I told him that I would wait.

Fresh

As soon as he clicked over, the fibbies zeroed in on me. They wanted me to get him started talking about drugs. My lawyer cut them off; told them to be patient and let me finesse the call. Before they could respond, we all heard the dial tone come through loud and clear. The nigga had hung up on me. I dialed the number back but it only rung. I tried again for thirty more minutes. He never answered. They racked their brains as to why he wouldn't pick back up. I had my own scenario but kept it to myself. Rah was letting me know that he knew I was behind that other fiasco.

* * * * *

(Princess)

"You think the nigga done forgot," Hood asked as he swigged from a bottle of Henny.

I glanced at the clock on the wall. We were in my office at the club. It was after three in the morning and Ivan still hadn't called to make good on our appointment. A check of the computer monitors let me know that Oz was almost finished ushering employees out the building. Nobody knew that I was there. I had told everybody that I was leaving earlier. Then after everyone saw me leave, I circled back and let myself into my office. I reached for my phone to text Ivan.

"Just be patient; he has a club to close himself. Give the man the time to get his business affairs in order. Trust me, it's no way he gonna pass up all this."

I teased as I stood up from his lap and shook my ass real quick. Hood had brought one of his goons up from down south to help out. The nigga was country as fuck and had a slow sexy country drawl. He looked too much like a pretty boy to be a killer. Hood slapped me on the ass and told me to chill out.

"Nah, dog, you need to chill with all of that drinking. Remember that we got work to do," his man warned.

My phone rang before Hood could reply. It was Ivan. The nickname that I had programmed for him read 'Clown.'

"Damn, I thought that you had forgotten about your girl."

"Never that ma, but I'm gonna have to beg off tonight. Some shit came up and…"

There was no way I was planning to let him get away tonight and instantly cut in. In my sexiest voice, I tried to sound as disappointed as possible. I told him that he needed to get his shit together because I was in the mood for some sex. I added that I had dressed in the Coogi dress that he liked with my ass hanging out just for him. I asked did he remember the dress.

"You mean the one with the Coogi logo across the ass, right?"

Fresh

"That's the one and I'll tell you another secret too. Before I came to work, I soaked in milk and honey just so I could taste real sweet for you," I purred.

"I want that too. I just wish you would've come to your senses on the other terms. You know I want you to be my girl."

I decided to switch it up a little. I didn't want the nigga getting too suspicious. In my B-more accent, I started to give him a piece of my mind.

"I can't believe this shit. I done went through all of this trouble for your ass. I'm all tipsy and shit. Why don't you just come through real quick for a little something? I'm too horny to go to sleep like this tonight," I chanted. "Now either you can come handle this itch, or I'll call somebody else to come take care of it."

The threat of somebody else getting the pussy did the trick. He gave in; told me that he would be by the club in twenty minutes. Hood offered me his tongue as a reward and whispered some promises in my ear for later. He got his boy's attention, before they stood and started laying plastic like painters.

"Now remember you guys that we need to find out who his partners are before we do anything," I reminded.

Hood nodded his dead and motioned towards his homie who promptly pulled out a blow torch and two pistols. He told me that getting the info out of yo wouldn't be a problem.

I left them to their business and retired to my bar to pour me one. I needed to loosen up a little to turn into the gangsta bitch that was needed of me tonight. After two shots, I was as loose as some over fucked pussy and ready to go. Headlights appeared on my parking lot surveillance screen and I started towards the front door.

"Places everyone; it's show time!"

Yo was headed towards the front door on his phone when I unlocked it for him. We started towards the office. He was busy telling his wife a bunch of lies and the time that he would be home to her. As soon as she agreed, he grabbed me in a bear hug.

"Come here and let me touch you."

I didn't resist. He turned me around and started to tongue me down as he groped on my ass. He kissed me like a little boy; wet and sloppy. Before I could resist, he reached for my skirt and lowered himself to his knees.

"Anxious aren't we," I asked as I stepped out of my thong.

For an answer, he merely turned me around and forced me to bend over. I grabbed the bar for support, thinking that letting him taste the pussy couldn't hurt. He had other plans though. Instead of attacking the pussy, he licked his fingers, spread my ass cheeks open and ran his tongue from the rooter to the tooter. Shit felt so good that I fucked around and knocked a bunch of glasses off the bar area.

The noise that I was making must've alarmed Hood because I heard footsteps approaching rapidly. A part of me got pissed with myself. Lord knows that I wanted to enjoy this oral situation but shit had to end. Poor Ivan was literally so far up my ass that he didn't even hear them coming. Twan smacked him with the burner to get his attention and he squealed like a hurt hyena. Hood came to check on me. After pulling down my dress, I immediately kicked Ivan in the head. I had to divert Hood's attention from what was going on when he entered the room.

"Take this faggot back to my office and watch the blood," I said before walking off.

The boys got Ivan situated while I poured myself a drink when we hit the office. Instead of Ivan arguing, he merely stared at me with hateful eyes.

"You thought I was some weak bitch that you and your boys could just muscle, huh," I asked as I planted my Christen Louboutin heel between his legs. He doubled over in pain. "Don't trip, because I'm not finished."

"Fuck you, you stinking pussy bitch," he said before hocking up a mouth full of spit and sending it in my direction.

Hood hit him with a right cross that sent him to the floor. Twan picked him up so Hood could hit him again. If the first punch didn't break his nose, then the second one did the trick. When Ivan finally looked up, his nose was lopsided and blood was squirting all over the place. Hood went into his pocket and produced the same thong that I had on earlier. He stuck it to Ivan's nose and squeezed.

"Smell that pussy! Do it smell? Do it," Hood asked.

Ivan let out a scream that could easily wake the dead. He started choking on his own blood. Afraid that he would kill him, Hood smacked him on the back and made him spit it out. Twan punched him in the gut to help him out. Ivan did as he was told. I sat at my desk and lit a blunt. I needed something to keep my hand from shaking. Hood bent down to eye level with Ivan.

"Listen up shorty. We can make this easy or hard. It's all up to you and how much pain you can take." He nodded at Twan who immediately lit his torch. Hood unbuckled Ivan's pants and fished his dick out. "My boy plans on roasting this little shit like a hotdog. You can avoid all that by simply telling shorty over there who your co-conspirators are that want to extort her. If your answers are satisfactory, we can get this shit over with and get home to our families. If not..."

He let his words trail off for effect. Twan stepped forward with his torch. Ivan yelled for everyone to chill. He was sweating like a pig while looking at me with a plea in his eyes. He asked if he was gonna die if he told the truth.

"Oh, you're definitely dying tonight playboy. The truth will only guarantee you a fast painless death. A lie will get you this." Hood motioned toward Twan.

Ivan yelled so loud when that heat touched his dick that the room stood still. I looked away; got a little noid that someone would heat that scream. Twan pulled the heat away for a moment and threatened to put it back.

"Hold up. Please, hold up," Ivan begged. "I...I got money; two mill. I have two million dollars stashed away at the Load It & Hold storage facility in Georgetown. Cash...and it's all yours. Plus, I'll give you the info that you want. Just don't kill me man..."

He started to cry like the bitch that I knew he was. Hood gave me a look and hunched his shoulders. Money wasn't our objective but two million was worth looking into. I winked at Hood and bent down close to Ivan.

"My boys want the money. All I want is the info and a guarantee that you'll leave town after we let you go tonight."

His dumb ass didn't have a choice but to bite the bait. After telling me that Baby Ray was behind the muscling thing, he didn't stop singing until the song was over. Hood extracted where Ray laid his head and some other info before ending with Ivan's storage details. With all that tucked away, Twan revealed one of the guns and handed it to me. I took it and pointed it at Ivan's dick.

"What the fuck did you plan on doing with that little shit," I asked before firing a shot that missed. I fired again and hit my mark. He screamed so loud that I put the next bullet in his head to shut him up.

Hood threw me Ivan's car keys and told me to pull it around back while they cleaned up. His boy Twan took the gun from me gently and asked if I was straight. I loved the way he said the word 'straight' and told him to repeat if for me on the way out the door.

Fresh

Chapter 12

(Prince)

"Prince," my mother yelled, taking my attention from the X-Box I was playing. "Boy, you better go out there and tell that girl to stop blowing that horn like we in the city before I do!"

I got up from the couch and stretched. My eyes went to the grandfather clock. It was fifteen after ten, which meant that I had only been playing the game for about an hour since we had returned from the polls. I headed to the front door. As soon as I opened the door, Asia climbed out the car and sprinted towards me chanting my name. It was a move I expected. Pia was still in her feelings about the Quita ordeal. In fact, she still wasn't speaking to me. I made up my mind to try and change all of that real quick.

Knowing that she was about to try to make a fast getaway, I swooped Asia up midway between her and the house then held up a hand to halt Pia. To my surprise, she waited. Instead of unlocking the passenger door, she rolled down the window.

"Grandma," Asia yelled while wiggling out of my arms.

Fresh

My mom waved to Pia; told her that she had breakfast on the stove and that she was welcome to join us. Pia declined claiming that she needed to get to the polls before it was too deep. During their exchange, I had managed to unlock the passenger door and slid into the seat. When my mother disappeared, the smile left from Pia's face.

"Did I say that you could sit in my car?"

"I thought I paid for this motherfucker," I answered sarcastically.

She started to respond, thought better of it and hit the unlock button. She asked me nicely to please let her leave. She repeated that she wanted to get to the polls before the lines got outrageous.

"Too late," I replied. "We went out there at four this morning and the lines were already ridiculous. We didn't get out of there until eight some time."

She exhaled loudly, checked the dashboard clock and mentioned that she wasn't gonna make it to school today. I nodded and then reached for her hand.

"Baby, don't you think that it's time we talked. I mean, I admit that I fucked up. You got every right to be pissed. I'm a bum. I need my asked kicked. I'll accept anything; any punishment that you want to dish out, but I can't accept you leaving me."

I had her attention. She ran her tongue over her teeth. I saw tears start to form in her eyes, but I didn't let up.

"We got to get through this ma. I been fucked up and sick this past week. I can't eat, sleep or nothing. I miss you ma," I pleaded.

"How many months is she Prince," she asked.

I kept eye contact. Her question was crucial. If I lied, she would probably get mad and shut me back out. If I told the truth, she would probably start asking more questions and only get angrier. I decided to tell here the truth and hope for the best.

"She's three months."

She flinched at my answer and immediately pulled her hand away from me. The tear that was threatening to fall, fell. I reached to wipe it away, but she avoided my touch.

"And she plans to keep it too?"

When I nodded that Quita was gonna keep the baby, the dam broke. Shorty started boo-hooing like a baby. I reached to hug her. She dipped like Ali in his prime and launched like five blows to my head. I ate those shits. I let her get them off before reaching and pulling her into my arms. I hugged her tight.

"I fucked up ma. I'm sorry though. Please forgive me. Please..."I begged.

She quit resisting and hugged me back; held me tighter than I held her. We stayed that way for at least five minutes. I didn't want to let go. She finally reached for the window button to let in some air and started wiping her eyes and getting herself together.

"You okay," I asked.

"I have no choice."

Before I could respond, Princess stuck her head out to speak and then announced that breakfast was ready. I told Pia to come in for a moment to eat and that I would accompany her to the polls when we were finished. She declined; said that she wanted to be alone to think. I nodded my head, just glad that she was at least talking to me again. I reached for the handle but she stopped me. She handed me a gift wrapped box along with Asia's book bag.

"Happy Birthday!"

I was surprised that she had thought about a nigga and immediately ripped open the box. Inside was a Cartier box. I whistled before I opened it and saw the iced out platinum Movado watch that I had checked out in New York. I reached in for a quick kiss. She didn't resist. I let her know that I loved the watch.

"I figured that you would." She put her car in gear. "Check the book bag and you'll find a gift for Princess in there."

Everyone was around the table preparing to eat the birthday breakfast that my mother had prepared for me and Twin. Of course Princess spotted the jewelry box and reached for it.

"Oooh, Cartier...somebody spent some money. Let me see!"

I sat down next to Asia and put an apron around her neck while the ladies inspected my gift. They were all in awe.

"Yeah, like I said, somebody spent some money. This is nice, isn't it Big Ma," Princess stated.

My mom agreed that it was nice then told us to dig in before her food got cold. She cooked this breakfast faithfully for us for as long as I could remember. No business was discussed while we grubbed. Instead, we chatted about the election and our hopes for a new President. After everyone was done, Princess rubbed her belly and promptly announced that she was ready for her gifts.

We all burst out laughing. Asia went for her book bag and presented both me and Princess a box from her. She had given us both keychains with her picture inside. My mother disappeared to the garage during our exchange. I reached for my jacket and handed Princess a gift. Her moth dropped to the floor. As close as we were, we had never exchanged gifts with one another.

"Oh, I didn't even think to get you anything..."

I waved her off and pointed to the box. She ripped it open and then screamed. Before I knew it, she was in my arms and planting kisses all over my face.

"Girl, chill the fuck out. They're only bracelets," I said with a laugh.

"I know but..." She stopped and wiped a tear from her face.

Mom came in and wanted to know what all the commotion was about. She saw the ten platinum bracelets I had just given my sister and smiled. She commented that I was always the thoughtful one and then rolled her eyes at Princess. She motioned for us to follow her to the garage. When I saw the two Bentleys that she had parked down there, I was the one who screamed and jumped into my mother's arms.

* * * * *

(T.O.)

Rah's young ass was starting to really piss me off. Not only was he not answering my calls, but he had also gotten so arrogant that he was just pressing the 'End' button and sending my shit straight to voicemail. That was a direct, 'fuck you.'

Yo was definitely in his feelings about the Lil' Thug situation. He sure couldn't have known about the DEA ordeal. Whatever the case, he pissed me off with that end call thing. That was something we do to bitches and since he was carrying me like a bitch, I suggested to the agents to wire me up and let me approach him head up. They were all for that and I was gonna throw in a bonus and try to discuss the Lil' Thug murder as well.

I and Bruh arrived at the mall a little after noon. The place was jammed packed with not only shoppers but voters also. Anticipating that this election was gonna be historic, the state had decided to place polls in the malls too. I myself had already voted this morning and sported my sticker proudly for everyone to see.

Bruh spotted Rah before we made it to his store. Evidently, he was about to open a second store because he was across from his store along with Diamond, watching workers hang a banner outside of a rental property. The sign announced the grand opening of 'The Spot: For Ladies' on December first.

Diamond was giving out orders as we approached. Shorty didn't even bat an eye when she saw me. It amazed me how us men got all jumpy and damn near gave ourselves away when we were wrong, but not females. A female could see their lover and keep it cool.

"And they say it's a recession," I joked good naturedly when Rah spotted me. I nodded at the opening sign. "Business must be good. Do I need to leave the cars alone and start pushing clothes?"

He was on the phone but did manage to say that he had learned from the best before motioning for us to follow him. When he got to his store, he told one of his workers to show us around while he went to the back to finish his call. After twenty minutes of waiting for the call to end, I got impatient. When he did finally come out, he looked annoyed to see us still out there.

"Let me find out that Tiffany couldn't interest you guys in anything," he asked before excusing his employee.

I told him that he knew I didn't come for a tie and left no room that I was playing when I said it. He looked around to make sure we didn't alarm any of his customers before asking me to follow him to his office. I noticed that his office was decked out like a mini apartment when I entered that joint. Not only did he have a desk fit for a president in that bitch, but he also had a pool table and a min bar present. The only thing he was missing was a bed and a jacuzzi. He leaned against his desk and asked me what he could do for me.

"I need work," I said flatly. "I want to double up on what we did last time."

He shook his head and headed for the bar; told me that he couldn't help me. I repeated what he had just said and asked him what type of games he was playing.

"No games Unc, when I say I can't help you, I mean it. I'm through with that shit…finished. I'm completely legit," he insisted while offering me a drink.

I looked him in his eyes. Either he was lying or deserved an award. I knew he was lying and decided to pull his card.

"Tell that shit to someone else. I was over in the hood and saw that things were up and running."

He shook his head again; told me that he had no idea what was going on in the hood these days. He said that he had left that to the wolves' months ago. He drained his glass and then headed towards his office door, indicating that the meeting is over.

I tried him again and asked if he had any knowledge of what happened to my rental property over in the hood. I even got specific and actually asked about the people that got killed and how my building was torched. My question got his attention. He didn't expect me to be so frank. He hesitated for a minute before putting a grin on his face. I think he even winked at me.

"I have no idea what you're talking about Unc. But you'll have to excuse me at the moment. I have to go get my vote on."

I walked out of his office with steam practically coming out of my nose. He slammed the door on my back. Bruh glared at me. When we got out into the car, I gave him his instructions.

"Get Bonnie on the line. Tell her that she is needed here in B-more, ASAP!"

* * * * *

(Raheem)

After T.O. left, Diamond and I went to go cast our votes. Afterwards, we grabbed a bite to eat together and then split up to run some errands. She was headed out to PG County to do some shopping with her cousins. I needed to go drop my jump off Kim some money to get her bills right. Nika had called earlier to confirm that she and Foxy were coming out tonight. With that said, I needed to get someone out to my bachelor pad to spruce up the place. Before any of this though, I needed to swing through the hood to pick up Prince's birthday gift.

Getting rid of the competition was proving to be a plus. Shop was up and running smoothly when I pulled up in the hood. Junkies were everywhere and the copping line was damn near a block long. I parked down the street and was met by three juvenile delinquents that were determined to replace me one day.

"You might as well hop back in your ride and get missing Rah," the oldest of the crew, Donte yelled. "It's hotter than a firecracker out here. Those people circling every five minutes. It's been that way since that shit happened around the corner."

I glanced at my watch. School wasn't even out, yet these three knuckleheads were posted as if they were holding shit down. I asked them why they weren't in school.

"Obama making history today; it's a national holiday. What, you didn't know," B.J. informed while giving the youngest of the crew, Lil' Tony, a high five.

I took a seat on the stoop to kick it with the youngins for a second. Donte and B.J. reminded me so much of me and Prince when we were their age. Before we were even in our teens good, we were already very knowledgeable of these streets and knew almost every trick of the trade. B.J. was my man Ace, who was currently doing a nickel in the feds for a gun case, little brother. I took a special liking to him and grabbed him in a headlock.

"I can't wait for your brother to get out. He gonna tighten your ass up."

He wiggled and squirmed away from my grip. After straightening his gear out, he popped his collar and stated that he too couldn't wait for his brother to come home. He said that after Ace was out, he maybe could make a decent living as a lookout or better. He told me that he could actually get paid for what he did all day for us for free.

Fresh

I stood up and shook my head. These niggas stayed on me about giving them lookout jobs, but I wasn't trying to hear of it. I had an eighteen and up policy that I had been enforcing since I opened up a couple of years ago. I dug in my pocket and produced three one hundred dollar bills. Three sets of hands reached for them. I held the money out of their reach.

"Since y'all want to work so bad, I got a gig for y'all boys. The job pays two hundred a piece a week. All y'all got to do is show up at my store every day at six to break down some boxes, get trash and maybe clean the glass. I'll even cop y'all some bus passes. It ain't much but it's what I pay my lookouts. So what do you think," I inquired.

They quickly agreed to my terms, snatched up their advance money and got missing. I headed up the block and ran into one of my workers.

"What's popping Tiny? I see y'all got it jumping around this piece," I related.

He didn't answer. His eyes were on the block and a black Bentley GT that was approaching us. The tints were dark and we couldn't see inside, but we did hear some Jezzy rattling the trunk. Tiny reached into his dip and moved in front of me.

"This is the third time this shit done rode through. I'm about to see what they are talking about," Tiny alerted.

Before he could pull out the weapon, the window to the GT came down and Prince stuck his head out the window. Tiny spoke first.

"Yo Prince, you need to quit playing." He showed him the gun. "Niggas nervous out here and playing for keeps."

I was moving towards the whip. I asked was this is new shit. For an answer, he jumped out nodding his head. The whip was cleaner than a bitch. He tossed me the keys.

"Bruh, she drives like a jet on wheels."

I jumped into the driver seat and started adjusting shit. Niggas came up to admire the whip. Moneybags was amongst the crowd. He gave Prince some dap first and then told me that he had something for me. I told him to grab that and I would pick it up after I circled the block.

Prince was right. His car drove like a dream. I was hating so hard, that I was tempted to drive straight to any lot and get me something new. I peeped my mom on a stoop and immediately pulled over to get her attention. Seeing her out here like this had no impact on me. She had been on the streets since I was a child. Still, I held a small grudge on the strength that she was weak and hadn't been there for me like she was supposed to.

After greeting Prince, she came around to give me a kiss. She asked why I had changed my number and not given it to her. I mumbled some lame excuse and waited for the punchline. She didn't let me down.

"Boy, dig in your pocket and give me something; some money, a few caps or something."

I opened my door and motioned for her to get into the back seat. I needed the house cleaned up and the few moments that it would take for her to do it, would be time for us together. On the drive out that way, I filled Prince in on the meeting that I had with T.O. earlier. He asked did I think T.O. was gonna be a problem.

"Fuck that old bastard. It's a wrap for him and he knows it. I gave him a pass with that shit he just pulled. Next time he's gonna get what his boys got last time," I boasted.

Prince produced a blunt from behind his ear and lit up. He told me to stay on point anyway; said that I had showed T.O. my hand today and probably had scared him. He stated that a scared nigga wouldn't hesitate to kill you. I decided to take heed to his warning.

* * * * *

(Princess)

"This shit free/ That means none for him/ And more for me/ I took something/ I'm gutter bitch/ Don't ever trust me dog…"

I rapped along with Yo Gotti as he and Gucci Mane performed at my birthday party. The place was packed and crunk. Unlike other times, I had the whole VIP on lock for my friends, the performers and the other celebrities that were in the building.

My mom was even in the house showing me love. That surprised the hell out of me. This wasn't her crowd and it showed. At the moment she was at the bar nursing a bottle of Cristal. I headed in her direction, grabbed her hands and rocked her to the beat of 'Freaky Girl.' It took her a minute to comprehend what the lyrics said and she promptly gave me the middle finger.

"Come on Ma and let's dance," I coaxed.

"Ain't nobody dancing to dis shit," she said while reaching for her bottle to pour herself another drink. "And I got your damn freaky girl."

I took the glass and bottle away from her. She was way wasted and it showed. I told her that it was time for me to find her a ride up out of here. She started to complain.

"Oh no you're not gonna just put me in the car with anybody. Where is my son at?"

Prince was on the dance floor enjoying his self and I had no plans to let her ruin that. I told her that I had a perfect driver for her as I steered her towards the front door. When we made it to the door, I asked my girl Jewel where T.T., the girl who I had hired to replace Oz's Judas ass, was at.

"She's in her office with Gucci's people. I think that it's a problem with the payout," she said while collecting from another customer.

The place was too packed for it to be a problem with the payout. The customer at the window got my attention before I could air my thoughts. My mother's ex, Darius, was in line a little overdressed, yet looking good in his Versace suit. My mother spotted him also and almost knocked me over trying to get to him. I grabbed her arm and whispered in here ear.

"I thought you were supposed to be mad with him," I reminded.

She didn't miss a beat as she moved pass me; told me that she was in fact mad and that she planned to get on his ass on the drive home. Thinking that he would be the perfect chauffer, I didn't object. Before they could leave, he handed me two envelopes with mines and Prince's name on them. Remembering that he had always given us gifts, I planted a kiss on his cheek and told him to drive safely.

I headed straight towards T.T.'s office once they were out of sight. When I stepped into the office, she stood and announced that I was the boss and could straighten everything out.

The guy that she was talking to was Gucci's manager. Yo had introduced himself earlier. He jumped to his feet and reminded me that he went by the name Nature Boy. On instinct, I zeroed in on him. He was cute in a pretty boy kind of way, but his skinny jeans were a definite turn-off. I stuck my hand out to greet him.

"I'm Princess, the owner of this establishment and birthday girl," I said with a wink. "What seems to be the problem back here?"

`Before he could respond the sound of the toilet flushing and the restroom door opening got my attention. Homeboy that stepped out the restroom made me do a double take. The nigga was fine as hell; put me in the mind of the reggae rapper, Sean Paul. Yo was pretty as hell; light skinned with some long ass corn rolls. My attraction to him was obvious and shocked me because I usually don't go for the light skinned ones, but this one...I don't know. Maybe it was the Jim Jones new growth that gave him an edge.

Nevertheless, I glanced behind him at the mirror to make sure I was on point. Pretty boy was on the phone but stopped in mid-sentence once he noticed me in the room. I almost pulled a white girl move and blushed once he pulled up his shades to get a better view.

"Yo Biz, we gonna holler more about this once I get back to the A. I gotta go right now. The gods must be on your boy side. Old girl who I told you I was scoping earlier, is in front of me now," he said into the receiver, while looking at me the whole time.

T.T. noticed the attraction in both of our eyes and promptly introduced the guy as Fire. She said that he was a producer with Gucci's camp and an obvious admirer. She told me that he had been back here hounding her to introduce him to me. She ended by giving him my resume.

I liked yo's walk immediately. He had a cocky ass walk; walked like he was in control. We call it swagger. He extended his hand but I spoke first.

"My girl said that you've been hounding her. Let me find out that you're the shy type," I asked with raised brows. "Can't approach a lady?"

He grinned, showing a mouth full of platinum jewelry; said that he had been scoping me from the sidelines. He explained that he was only being patient until the opportunity presented itself. He wouldn't release my hand as he spoke. I didn't want him to. He noted that while he was scoping me, he noticed that I didn't leave the side of some dude wearing Coogi. I racked my brain for who could he be talking about. Both Rah and Prince had on Coogi tonight and I had been chilling with them.

"It's a lot of Coogi out there. I hope you're not talking about the dude in the black sweater," I asked.

"Black jeans, Gucci shades and golf balls in his ears," he nodded. "I figured that he was your man and didn't want to intrude."

I explained to him that Prince wasn't my man. I told him that we were celebrating our birthday together. He seemed relieved to hear this. His man Nature Boy cut us off before we got too cozy.

"Yeah, yeah, yeah...we've heard it all before." He turned to Fire. "I'm hating nigga because I saw her first. But since it's obvious that you have her attention, I'm just gonna state my business and get out of y'all way."

He went on to say that So Icey Entertainment was currently being watched by the IRS and needed to be paid by check, so that good old Uncle Sam could get his cut. His request surprised me. Most entertainers wanted to be paid in cash just to avoid the IRS. Nevertheless, I merely nodded; told him that a check wouldn't be a problem. I asked him to be patient while I slid next door to get my checkbook.

I stepped out into the hallway and was delighted to find out that Fire was behind me. Once we stepped into my office, I nodded towards my bar. I let him know that I liked Goose and he could help himself to whatever. While he poured us drinks, I hit the safe.

Fresh

"So you're a producer with Gucci's camp," I asked.

"Actually, I'm independent. I'm currently working with Gucci on his next album. We were in the studio yesterday getting it in when he suggested that I join him tonight," he relayed.

I nodded and told him that the rumor was that the real money went to the producers. He laughed before presenting me with my drink and promptly perching his ass on the corner of my desk. He produced a blunt from behind his ear and asked if it was okay to spark. I nodded an okay.

"Writing and producing pays the bills. Fortunately, I do both."

"Fire...never heard of you before but then again, I can't name too many producers as is. Just Blaze...and maybe Kanye is it."

He nodded and said that he wasn't as commercial as he planned to be, but mentioned that I might have heard some of his work. I raised an eyebrow. He proclaimed that he had produced the 'Rollin' beat for Gucci.

"Is you rollin? Bitch I might be!" I hummed and then alerted him that the song was my favorite.

He raised his glass in salute after passing me the blunt. I asked him had he worked with any other famous people. He squinted as if in thought.

"Shit, basically I fuck with a lot of south people but I'm not biased. Let's see...I've worked with Luda, Jeezy, Ross, etc. I've written for Keisha Cole, Rihanna, Mario, Kelly from Destiny's Child."

"Watch out now. Those are some big names. Let me find out you on your Neyo shit," I teased.

He laughed and stood to look at the pictures of me and some of the entertainers who had been in the club. I was through with the check but not ready to leave his presence. He must've felt the same way because he had an idea.

"How about, you go pay Nature while I head to the bus to get some more weed. Then, we meet up out front and you take me to see your city."

I didn't hesitate before standing and telling him that I would be beside the Barbie Mobile out front in ten minutes.

* * * * *

(Gloria)

"Good God Almighty...Father in heaven...Forgive me please," I prayed.

At the moment, I was at Darius' house on his couch while he knelt in front of me. My dress was hiked up around my waist and his face was buried in my nana. He was doing what he did best.

How I got here, I don't know. As promised, I cursed his ass out good on the drive to his penthouse. Of course, he tried to deny the white girl, but all that changed once I whipped out my evidence. After seeing that, he admitted to the fling but tried to down play it as a one night stand.

Hearing him confess made me feel good in a way. After all, it's been me who's been fowl throughout this relationship. Overall, Darius is a good, God fearing man. He's practically worshipped the ground that I've walked on for as long as I can remember. Throughout all of that time, I've never really belonged to him. So hearing him admit his shortcomings consoled my guilty conscious.

Shit, guilt conscious plus the Cristal was what led to me to his 16th floor penthouse. I was in need of a tune up anyway.

When I came, I came hard; almost violently. That felt so good that I shoved him from between my legs with enough force to give him whiplash. That didn't stop him though.

"NO…No more," I panted. "I can't take anymore. I need….I need a minute. Go get me something to drink."

He got up to go handle that like I knew he would. I headed towards his bedroom and started to shed my clothes. I wanted to get in the shower; needed the cold water to calm my nerves. He met me in his restroom with my water. I was on the toilet.

"You feel like a bath," he asked.

"A shower will do. Do you plan on joining me?"

That was all of the urging that he needed. He was naked and in the shower, before I could even wipe my ass. I got up to be nosy and checked his medicine cabinet. I noticed that instead of the two that normally rested there, there were now three toothbrushes. I opened a drawer and found a hairbrush. It was full of blond hair.

"Hey you...you coming in or what," he asked from behind the curtain.

I sat the brush down and stepped in the shower. Evidence was everywhere. The scent of peaches and strawberries was in the air. I saw Nivea and Aveeno lotion; Bath and Body shower wash was in reaching distance. I grabbed it and squirted half the bottle on my rag. Let him explain that to the bitch.

My mind was made up to carry my ass home by the time I finished cleansing myself. When I tried to step out of the shower, he changed my mind by grabbing my hand and placing it on his hard dick. Call me weak or a freak. I say I'm just horny because I instantly lifted a leg and bent over slightly for easy access. He entered me roughly and abruptly.

"Oh baby, that's what I'm talking about," I moaned.

Fresh

He found a good rhythm and started to stroke. I closed my eyes and held on for the ride. He was compassionate and unselfish; trying to make sure that I came before him. He was gonna regret his little tactic today though, because as soon as I got my nut, I slipped out of his embrace and exited the shower.

"Hold up...where are you going," he asked while stepping out behind me.

I scooped up my panties and headed for the bedroom where my other clothes were at. He followed. I pointed to the bed and told him that I was headed to get some ice. He grinned and nodded.

As soon as he turned his head, I grabbed my dress and heels and headed for the living room. After slipping into my Carolina Herrera get up, I made a dash for the kitchen to retrieve a spare set of his car keys. With the keys, Jimmy Choos in hand, I headed for the elevator.

The elevator arrived just as Darius stuck his head out the door to ask what was wrong. Luckily, he was naked and couldn't run after me. I ignored him and stepped inside the elevator. It seemed like it took forever for me to make it to the ground floor. However, when I did make it there, I wasn't prepared for the sight in front of me.

Engaged in a lip lock that would make Angelina Jolie jealous were Raheem's girlfriend,

Diamond, and a man old enough to be her father. After a closer look at her companion, I knew who he was immediately.

"Gloria," the man asked.

"Tyrell?"

"Ms. Gloria," Diamond asked in shock before realizing that I and her date were on a first name basis. She glanced at him and then back at me. "Ms. Gloria, this is not what it looks like."

I held up a hand to stop her. There was no need for excuses. Even Ray Charles could tell what I had just seen. Still, I had problems of my own at the moment. I glanced at the elevator monitor and saw that Darius was on the way down. Tyrell noticed my glance and the shoes in my hand and asked was everything okay with me. I told him that all was good before stepping past him. Diamond said something to my back, but I didn't wait around to hear it.

* * * * *

(Raheem)

I awoke to the sound of banging on my front door. I was lying between both Foxy and Nika. We were all naked. It turns out that Nika wasn't bullshitting when she told me that her friend wanted to fuck me. However, hearing someone knocking like the law spooked everyone.

Fresh

"Oh shit, sounds like somebody's in trouble," Foxy yawned.

Nika was on her feet and searching for her clothes. She started accusing me of lying about this house being safe. I ignored her and began to dress myself. I wasn't necessarily worried because few people actually knew about this apartment and Diamond wasn't one. Prince walked inside confidently once I made it to the door, with Aunt Glo tagging along. Her presence raised a red flag.

"What's going on family?" I accepted the cup of Starbucks coffee that Aunt Glo offered. "Is everything okay?"

My aunt roamed and let her eyes inspect my bachelor pad. After spotting the trail of clothes that the girls and I left behind last night, she asked me to please get rid of my company so that we could discuss family business. I headed for the room. I told the ladies that I was gonna take a ride with my fam and that they were welcomed to stay. I even offered to bring them back breakfast. Nika was spooked and declined for the both of them. I knew she wouldn't be here when I got back.

I convinced Glo that taking a ride around the block would be better and she agreed. Outside, they were traveling in two separate cars. I hopped in the Escalade with Aunt Glo and got comfy. However, I wasn't prepared for the bomb that she dropped on my lap once we got in traffic. The news and eyewitness account of what she saw that morning almost floored me. I had to take a few deep breaths to find my voice before I spoke.

"You said that you know this dude she was with," I asked while contemplating murder.

She nodded her head for an answer. She said that she knew dude pretty well and that he actually used to run with Prince's dad back in the day.

I reached for the cigarette that she was smoking; needed to inhale something. I usually smoked tree when like this, but unfortunately, none was on hand so I had to make do. After I got myself together, I asked for the guy's name.

"His name is Tyrell. I can't remember his last name. But make no mistake nephew, that man is not to blame. I'm pretty sure that Diamond was a willing participant, so don't go doing anything stupid."

I tuned her out. Even though she was right about Diamond being responsible, I was still in kill mode. I immediately reached for my phone and turned the power on. My call log was over flooded. A quick scroll let me know that most of the calls were from Diamond. I pressed the send beside the word 'Wifey.' She answered on the first ring already on the defensive. She said that she had been calling all night and wanted to know why I hadn't been answering my phone.

Fresh

I wanted to laugh. This was typical Diamond. Shorty was using reverse psychology, probably trying to see what I knew. I exhaled and spoke slowly so she could hear me loud and clear.

"Listen up and listen real good. I'll be home in the next hour. When I get there you better not be in my residence. Use this hour to pack and remove your shit from my house. You can keep everything that I've bought you. Just don't touch any of my furniture or appliances. You can use my truck but be sure to have it returned by dark. I sincerely advise that you are not there when I arrive."

She started to try to explain but I hung up in her ear. I reached for Aunt Glo's purse and retrieved another cigarette. She reached for my hand and squeezed it tight. I guess she knew that I was hurting at the moment. Before long, we were gaining access to an underground garage. I noticed that we were out Butcher's Hill. She parked the truck beside a black Maybach, grabbed her purse and we exited the vehicle. Parked beside the Maybach was a red Ferrari Spider. A platinum Porsche was beside the Spider. It was then that reality hit me.

"Hold up Aunty. You said that dude name is Tyrell, right?" She nodded her head. "Tyrell Owens, like the football player," I specified.

She searched he memory quickly and then shrugged; said she couldn't recall his last name at the moment. I described T.O. to her. She agreed with my description. She asked me how I knew yo. I didn't answer; couldn't answer. My blood was on overdrive. I started having flashbacks to the way that yo used to look at Diamond. I thought about how he just practically gave her the Benz. All the slick comments; and to make matters worse, the bitch been playing me all along. I literally punched the window out of the Ferrari and set the alarm off.

Blood started pouring from my open wound. Prince came to check on me. I backed away from him. My phone was vibrating in my pocket. I answered in gorilla pimp mode.

"Bitch, you are wasting valuable time by calling me. You only have 45 minutes left," I bellowed and hung up.

Aunt Glo grabbed me by the elbow and escorted me to Prince's Magnum. After I was in the car, I dialed Moneybag's number and told him to have Tiny meet me at the shop shortly.

Fresh

Chapter 13

(Gloria)

It surprised me when it took the prison guards all day to bring King into the lawyer/client visiting room. Whatever the case, my mouth started to water once I laid eyes on that tall dark specimen of a man. As usual, his prison clothes were pressed to the tee. I hated to admit it but he made those khakis look like they were Stacy Adams or some shit.

"You may have to excuse me if I smell like garlic, but you caught me at a bad time. I was in the middle of a culinary class when they told me you were out here. I didn't even have time to shower or anything," he explained while taking a seat.

I told him that an apology wasn't necessary. I asked what the class was cooking today. When he mentioned that they were cooking seabass with okra marinated in white wine, my mouth started to water again. I moaned out loud.

"Now that sounds delicious. Promise me that you will cook for me like that when you come home."

He leaned back in his chair and winked. He told me that he had me when he got out. I told him that I was gonna hold him to that one, and then asked how he managed to get both rum and white wine into the facility. He commented that it wasn't much that he wasn't able to get up in the prison.

"Is that right," I teased. "Well, enlighten me. Why haven't you gotten 'me' up in this piece?"

He laughed and stated that he was working on it. My mind drifted back to the days that we did indeed used to get busy. That was when he was at Butner in North Carolina. That place was crawling with greedy C.O.'s who didn't mind making a fast buck. The real problem there was that it was flooded with snitches. It turned out that a female C.O. that was on our payroll was a fucking snitch. The bitch got loose lipped about our business and all went to hell. A full investigation was launched but turned up nothing. King got shipped here to Petersburg and the rest is history. That incident was the reason that we were watched so heavily during these meetings.

"Patience Mama, this will be all over, and I'm talking real soon." I grinned as he reassured me.

"Do you have an exact date?"

"I wish I did. I do know that Obama was elected two weeks ago and that the clock is ticking. The white man is out and anxious to fuck America over one more time. I'm not sweating it. I should be home any day now," he promised.

I nodded and reached for my pad and pencil. I needed to get to the real reason for this meeting. I told him that I needed to go over a few things with him; like did he have any specific needs or place that he wanted to spend his first week at. I told him that I already been online looking at rental properties.

"It would be nice to go up to the mountains somewhere; Alaska or maybe Colorado. It really doesn't matter. I just want it to be cold, secluded and quiet. I want you all to myself that first week," he said with a wink.

I winked back and told him that I had the perfect place for what he wanted. It was a ski resort out in Idaho that I had taken ma and the kids a few years back. The place was a wonderland and perfect for what he had in mind. My next question was where he wanted to go after Idaho and to keep in mind that our children should be invited to this one.

"That's what's up. I've been checking out a lot of magazines. How about us all going down to Florida; South Beach? We can rent a house on Star Island. I want to party with Puffy and them."

I nodded and took notes; informed him that his idea sounded expensive but that we could afford it. Next I told him that his daughter had offered to purchase him a vehicle; said that according to her, he could have any make and model that he wanted. I suggested that since she was paying, he should ask for a Benz. I told him that she could well afford it and reminded him that she was making a mint off that club of hers. In fact, her business was the only business we had that was turning a profit already.

"That's my baby, Glo. I told you she could handle it. You just had to give her some space and let her do her," he said before taking my hand. "Did I ever tell you thank you for raising my two lovely kids?"

I nodded because it was true that he had in fact been thanking me since I had the kids. I reached in my briefcase and produced a tape measurer next. I needed to get his measurements so I could do a little shopping for him.

"Tell my daughter that a grey Silverado will do fine; and while you're delivering messages, tell my son that a visit would be nice."

I told that him message would be relayed and took a seat. We spent the rest of the visit discussing the kids and businesses that we were involved in. When I spoke about Rah, it reminded me of Diamond's infidelity and I told him about that. When I mentioned Tyrell's name, his eyes clouded over and I became suspicious. Knowing this man like I did, made me curious. I asked him what was wrong. He assured me that all was well.

"And while we are on old friends Bae, I need you to look up one of my old ones for me. His name is Larry Bell. Last I heard that he was still in

Baltimore somewhere. That was a close friend of mines. If you find out something, let me know."

* * * * *

(Princess)

Fire got his first strike when he didn't meet me at the airport in Atlanta himself. Instead, I was met by a big bodyguard type, bearing a sign with my name on it. He introduced himself as Ike and explained that Fire was stuck in the studio and couldn't get away. He emphasized Fire's apologies and stressed that his boss had promised to make everything up to me with a special evening that he had planned. With that said, he loaded my Tumi luggage, a gift from cousin rah for my birthday, into a tricked out Navigator and we were on our way.

It wasn't my first time in Atlanta, but Ike still took it upon himself to point out what was what. After a twenty minute drive, we pulled into a gated community that boasted houses to some of the city's biggest stars. Ike pointed out Jeezy's and Whitney's shit. These houses made my mother shit look like a shack. In fact, you couldn't even call these cribs houses. These were what one would call estates. I wondered if Fire lived out this way. My suspicions were quickly confirmed once Ike whipped into a driveway in which the crib was even as lavish as the house he had pointed out earlier that belonged to Darkchild.

Fresh

"This is very nice," I commended while trying not to sound too excited. "How many bedrooms does it have?"

"I think the main house got like 6 or 7 bedrooms. I know that the guest house out back has 3 bedrooms."

If Fire was trying to impress me by bringing me here, then he was doing a damn good job. The house sat far back from the main street. It even had a mini pond in the front. The driveway was circular and decorated with an array of expensive cars. The most impressive of the fleet was a pearl white Phantom. A red Maserati, a champagne Range and a Maybach was out there to keep it company.

Ike grabbed my luggage and led me to the front door where a Mexican maid greeted us. From where I stood in the foyer, I could basically see the whole house. Everything was done up in a bachelor black. On the walls he had his wall of fame. From just a glance, I noticed nine platinum plaques and just as many gold ones.

"You want me to put your luggage in the boss's room or do you prefer your own," Ike asked with a sneaky leer.

I told him that my own would do just fine. He walked over to an elevator and deposited all my shit aboard. When I gave a curious look, he informed me that the maid would handle that and directed to the area of the studio.

As I expected, the studio was located in the basement; and when I say studio, I don't mean your basic layout. The nigga Fire had a state of the art joint built complete with a soundproof booth and all. I could tell that he dropped a mint on this impressive bit of equipment. Six niggas were in one room playing Madden on a big screen. Fire sat in a room overlooking the booth behind a beat board. He was busy nodding his head and pushing buttons. A nerdy white guy who looked totally out of place sat beside him. In the booth, rapping while smoking a blunt was Jadakiss.

`"Damn…" Fire said while sounding frustrated. "My fault Jada, that was me that time. Start from 'We in the streets; ready…'"

Jada took off his headphones and nodded in my direction. The white boy did a double take. Fire broke out in a grin and greeted me with a hug. He wanted a kiss.

"Muah," Jada mimicked, doing his signature ad lib. "Am I glad to see you; now maybe this workaholic will give a nigga a break?"

He got up and came out the booth. Fire introduced me as his female friend that he had been telling him about. He turned to me and told me that Jada was the reason he didn't pick me up personally from the airport. He then pointed at the white boy and introduced him as Mike the Technician.

"Nice to meet all of you guys," I greeted as I sat and crossed my legs ladylike.

Jada took a seat across from me on the couch. Mike excused himself to the restroom. Fire took a seat next to me and inquired about my flight. I told him that everything was comfy and thanked him for the first class comp.

"So you're the lady who owns that exclusive club in D.C.," Jada asked as he snapped his finger. "What's the name of that joint?"

"Princess's Palace," I answered. "We tried to book you to perform last month when we heard you was gonna be in the area, but your people gave us the run around."

"That would be my manager/cousin Belinda that you talked to. You have to excuse her. If she wasn't fam, I would fire her ass personally," he joked as he passed fire the blunt. "Anyway, she did mention that y'all called. I'll tell you what though. I'll be back in your area promoting this new album soon, so maybe we can make that happen then."

We exchanged personal contacts before he returned to the booth. Mike resurfaced ready to work. Fire offered his credit card and a driver for me to shop, but I declined. I told him that I would rather watch him work. That seemed to please him.

Jada was right when he said that Fire was a workaholic. It took almost an hour just to lay down one verse to Fire's specifics. Jada repeated the verse so many times that I memorized it myself. They took another smoke break and got back to work. Before leaving, Fire offered an explanation but I wouldn't hear it. I told him to handle his business because I wanted him all to myself tomorrow.

He agreed to my terms and disappeared back behind his boards. The session lasted another two hours before they finally got it right. After everyone was gone, Fire walked me to my room and told me to have a nice night. I closed the door behind him with thoughts of what it would be like to be his girl in my head.

* * * * *

(T.O.)

"All I want to know is how are you gonna blame me? You act as if it was my intentions for us to get caught."

I was at my D.C. dealership on the horn with Diamond. We hadn't talked since the night we were spotted at my crib. Shorty was on some shit like it was my fault.

"No, I'm not saying that you meant to get us caught. I am saying that I think shit has been moving too fast and I'm the one who is losing over this shit. He kicked me out T.O., for Christ's sake! I'm back with my mother."

I cut her off and offered to put her in her own crib again. Fuck it; making her my mistress could only be a plus. With her in a crib that I pay for would only grant me unlimited access. She gave me an aggravated sigh and started mumbling to herself. I glanced at my watch. The bitch Bonnie was coming through to test-drive a whip and discuss business. We needed to speak about this Rah situation. For some reason, it was taking her a long time to put his ass in the dirt and I felt that I needed to light a fire under her ass. My saleslady stuck her head inside my office and told me that she was here. I told her to put some tags on an Audi and tell the customer that I would be there in a sec.

I gave Diamond back my attention. I told her that we needed to get together and talk all this out. She agreed to meet me at a restaurant later and we hung up.

Bonnie was waiting in a white Audi when I got outside. As soon as she got into traffic, she got right down to business.

"I finally made contact two days ago. Like I told you before, the guy has been holed up in his apartment for the last two weeks. I finally laid eyes on him the other night."

Evidently Rah was as hung up over Diamond as she was over him. I could imagine what he was going through though. I had been involved with shorty for not even six months and she already had a tight hold on me. I turned my attention back to Bonnie.

"You should have hit him when you saw him then."

She shook her head in the negative; told me that she liked to survey her victims before moving on them. I asked her where he went when he did leave the building.

"He left his apartment and picked up a male and a small child. They went to a local Chucky Cheese for lunch. While the child played, they talked.

My mind contemplated who Rah's companion was and settled on his cousin Prince. If my assumptions were correct, his cousin was involved with this dope shit also. If that was the case, he needed to be dealt with in the same fashion as his cousin.

"You should have hit them both then. In fact, I have more work for you since you're already in the city. Rah's out top priority right now, but this other business is just as important," I advised.

She mumbled something about me having trouble in paradise and accelerated the vehicle even more.

* * * * *

(Prince)

"And daddy, my grandma Gloria said that I could go with her to get my nails done too," Asia announced proudly.

Fresh

I nodded and wiped the ice cream from her lip at the same time. We were at the food court in the mall enjoying some us time like always. She was talking a mile a minute as usual. My mind was on her mother Pia. Shorty had been playing some fucked up games with a nigga. I had made no progress at restoring our relationship and it wasn't because I hadn't been trying. In a nut shell, shorty was just on some other shit.

For instance, today she had called me out of the blue and asked me to get Asia from daycare. She said that she had something to do. When I asked what was up, she got offensive; went into how she wasn't my girl anymore and didn't have to explain. I let her win that one and dropped the conversation. Later, I asked Asia what her mother's plans were for the day. She told me something about Pia having a date. I drilled her softly for more info but didn't get far. When I called Pia to inquire, she sent my calls straight to voicemail.

"Daddy, did you hear what I just said," Asia asked, taking me out of my thoughts.

I confirmed that she had my attention when she really didn't. She quizzed me on the topic and realized that I wasn't listening. My punishment for ignoring her was to get her another sundae. Before we could get up and make that happen, I felt a pair of hands cover my eyes and knew instantly that it was Quita from the $800 perfume I smelled.

"Guess who?"

I chuckled and she released me. My eyes went straight to Asia. She was busy giving Quita the evil eye. I had no doubt that she remembered shorty from the encounter at the mall. My baby wasn't a slouch. She probably knew that this was the same girl who was the reason for me and her mother's problems. She surprised me when she asked Quita's name.

"Her name is Samone," I lied before Quita could say anything. I didn't miss the instant look that Quita gave me also.

Asia gave me a stare as if she knew something was up. Before she could ask any more questions, I dug in my pocket and pulled out some money.

"Here honey; why don't you go buy your own sundae and when you come back, we will go buy 'Toys R Us' and pick you up something." Asia wasn't buying the con though.

"I thought that you said that I couldn't have any more toys until after Christmas," she reminded.

I gave her a look and told her that I was the boss and could break any rule that I pleased. She heard the aggression in my voice and took the money. As soon as she had disappeared, I turned back to Quita. She didn't look happy. This was the second time that I had choked up on her.

"Oh, so now I'm Samone," she started.

Fresh

I reached for her hand but she snatched it away. I argued that Asia knowing her real name wasn't too wise right now. I told her that if Pia found out that we were all here, she would probably get on some keeping Asia away from me type shit.

She studied me for a long time probably to see if I was serious. Instead of going ghetto on me like I expected, she peeped Asia returning and simply walked off. When I started to follow her, Asia grabbed my arm and stopped me.

"Where are you going, daddy? Remember... 'Toys R Us' is this way."

* * * * *

(Raheem)

The bitch Diamond had me in the Matrix for real. Since our fallout, I've been in slow motion. A nigga can't eat. I toss and turn all night. My dick won't get hard for any of my jump-offs. Real talk, my stomach literally aches at the thought of my situation. It seems like all I've been able to do lately is drink and smoke.

Tonight, I have company though and hope to change all that. Kim came over earlier to cook and clean for a nigga. She's in the shower at the moment cleaning that twat for a nigga while I sat at my computer checking out real estate. Living in this condo was starting to fuck with my head; too many memories of Diamond.

Of course shorty has been on my dick since the breakup; calling all times of the night, popping up at the store and even got a call from a neighbor telling me that she was parked outside of the crib one night on some stalker shit. Nevertheless, that bitch could freeze to death out there for all I care. As far as I'm concerned, it's a wrap for that chicken.

Speaking of the devil, my email logo bleeped across the screen while my phone vibrated on the table. Both were from her and read identical. She wasn't saying much; a bunch of begging and shit. She had the nerve to bring five different scenarios when she either caught me cheating or heard that I was. She claimed that she had been faithful to me for the last five years and pleaded that I take that into consideration. She ended by saying that she knew of the chick that I had over at the moment and that she was even willing to forget that if I would reconsider.

"Get the fuck out of here," I said out loud as I reached for my blunt. "Who the fuck you think I am?"

"I know you're not talking to yourself are you," Kim asked from behind.

I spun around in my chair. Shorty was dressed to impress in nothing but a small teddy. She was gorgeous too. I could see straight through that shit and all her goodies were out. In her hand, she had a black bag. I pointed at the screen to indicate what I was talking to myself about.

"Dang, she is crazy. How do you think that she knows I'm here," Kim questioned as she went to close the blinds.

I watched her ass as she retreated. The teddy barely covered that ass. Watching it jiggle got a rise out of me. I stood up. I told her that I wasn't tripping over Diamond at the moment. I patted my lap. She came over and sat astraddle me. I'm not even big on kissing but tonight, she caught me in my feelings. She accepted my affection, started grinding on my lap and hugged me tight. I instantly scooped her up and headed for the bedroom.

She took over once we arrived there and pushed me on the bed. First she dimmed the lights and found my remote. R Kelly's 'TP2' came blasting from my speakers. I immediately started to come out of my boxers and shit while she sashayed back over. Once I was naked and comfortable, she emptied the contents of her black bag out on the bed. Inside, she had only one item. I reached for the tube and read.

"Dickalicious," I asked with a raised brow.

We both burst out laughing. She snatched the bottle from my hand. I asked what the tube was all about. She got serious when she answered.

"As you probably already know, my head game is not up to point," she admitted while giving me a suspicious look. I guess she wanted me to tell her that she wasn't amateur night, but I kept my poker face. "Anyway, Tia and I were at 'Goodies' the other day and I thought of you when I saw this. I guess I want to please you."

She opened the tube and tasted a little bit. Afterwards, she jumped up and exited the room. She returned with a blunt and a fresh drink of Goose.

"It doesn't taste too bad. It got my mouth wet as a bitch." She grabbed my finger and stuck it in her mouth. I smiled. She lit my blunt and stuck it in my mouth. "You just relax; lie back like a rich nigga and let mama practice on you. Can you do that?"

For an answer, I got comfy. No sooner than she started working me over, my cell rang. It was a Project Pat tone that I only gave to one nigga. I instantly reached for my phone while trying not to disturb shorty.

"What it do, little nigga," I asked Tiny.

"It ain't too much; I was calling to let you know that I had your boy in sight. He's at a restaurant with a bitch. The problem is that the bitch got a strong resemblance to your bitch," he informed with a laugh. "Real talk, shorty and Diamond could go for twins."

I interrupted Kim from what she was doing and sat up. The nigga Tiny didn't know the reason that he was ordered to off T.O. Evidently, he had his people fucked up though. I had just received an email from Diamond not even ten minutes earlier. Shorty had to be somewhere near a computer, or… I stopped in my tracks. These fucking I-phones are amazing these days. I got out of bed real quick and stared searching my closet for something to wear.

"Where you at my nigga," I asked him.

"I'm sitting outside this restaurant downtown named Rizzo's. They got a table near the window. I'm checking yo out right now as we speak."

I told him to stay right where he was at and that I would be there in ten minutes. He tried to tell me that he could handle his job, but I wasn't trying to hear it. I wanted to; needed to see this shit for myself.

It took me less than ten minutes to suit up in black. Kim sat on the bed with a crazy look on her face. I gave her an apologetic gesture and told her that duty was calling and that I needed her car to be on some incognito shit. She didn't argue. Fifteen minutes later, I was parking the car around the corner from where Tiny was parked.

I found him posted in a black Geo directly across from the restaurant. I checked out our surroundings. Rizzo's was upscale all the way; even had valet parking and shit. I spotted T.O. and Diamond immediately. They were posted on the second floor, smiling and giggling like they didn't have a care in the world. I turned to Tiny who was watching me closely, no doubt putting two and two together.

"Give me your heat, bruh," I demanded.

He didn't budge. Instead, he shook his head and asked what I had planned.

"Just give me the joint, yo. I ain't going out like this. I'm walking in this bitch and busting this nigga head," I said as I reached for the gun.

He easily moved it away from my reach. I eyed him to let him know that I was serious. He shook his head; told me that he wasn't letting me go out like that. He added that I was in my feelings and not thinking right.

A part of me wanted to fight, but his words hit close to home. He knew he had my attention and elaborated more. He said that I had too much going to go out like that; told me that I was paying him too much money and to let him do his job. I couldn't argue with that. Instead, I told him that I wanted T.O.'s ass dead tonight and asked him for his plan.

"Shit, I got like three straps on me; this mac right here; got the chopper in the trunk and a fucking high powered rifle joint too. Right now, I'm contemplating going up on that roof right there and taking a shot," he confessed while pointing. "The problem is all that traffic with the valet shit. I'm scared somebody might see me with that big ass shit."

I scanned our surroundings. The roof could work, but like he said, the traffic was too thick. The only way he was getting to that nigga tonight was either to catch him as he waited on his car and pull a drive by or to follow him home. Tiny studied me for a minute and finally nodded.

"I can see the valet joint working but I'm not with a drive by; too many bystanders. Plus, we got to make our shot count. If we miss, shit can get hectic out here," he foresaw as he shook his head. "We got the element of surprise. I'm hitting this nigga tonight. Fuck it, you gonna have to drive though. When they come out, I'm blending in with the crowd and going for mines. Do you want shorty hit too?"

I told him that hitting shorty was his call. My main concern was old boy's snake ass. He nodded his head and climbed out. I knew I was signing old girl's death certificate, but I didn't give a fuck. She wanted to play in the big leagues so she was getting her just do.

After Tiny disappeared from my view, I turned my attention to Diamond and got even madder. I reached for the ashtray. It was empty. I cursed out loud and remembered that Tiny was drug-free. Yo was on point and about his business. With that thought on my mind, I decided to wipe the car down for fingerprints while I waited. I was so in my feelings earlier that I forgot to bring some gloves.

I found a cloth in the glove compartment and started to clean up. A knock on the passenger window startled me. It was a white woman. She looked like a bum. I rolled the window down. She held up a cigarette.

"I'm sorry to bother you man, but I need a light," she asked in a frantic voice.

"Get the fuck away from my car bitch! Hell no, I don't have a light," I yelled and started to roll my window back up.

"Well, fuck you then!"

Her response startled me. I looked up and found myself staring down the barrel of a silenced pistol. I didn't even hear the first shot.

* * * * *

(T.O.)

Right when I got Diamond to agree to come back to my place, a commotion started outside causing some of the customers to approach the window to be nosey. Of course, Diamond's ass wanted to be nosey too. Out the window, we saw a lot of people crowding around a car.

"I wonder what the hell is going on out there," she asked in a concerned voice.

Fresh

I searched the restaurant for the manager. He was busy scolding a waiter. The waiter started closing the window so the commotion outside wouldn't disturb the customers. When he neared our table, I asked him what the problem was. His answer was that he had no idea and tried to see if everything was satisfactory with our meal.

"Everything was delicious," I assured as I handed a twenty and our valet receipt.

The waiter nodded and hurried away. Diamond started to fidget with her phone while mines vibrated in my pocket. It was Bruh.

"Yeah?"

"It's done. I just heard from your girl," was his reply.

I smiled instantly. I asked him whether she let on to how or where the assassination took place.

"You know she didn't elaborate," he responded. "All I got was a text asking to transfer the rest of the money. She did ask for a package on that other thing that y'all discussed; whatever the fuck that supposed to mean."

The other package was for Rah's cousin Prince. That one would have to wait for a couple of days. I told him to go ahead and wire her the other half of her paper. When he hung up, I took another peek out the window. The ambulance had arrived.

"I wonder what's going on," I asked out loud.

The waiter arrived with our coats and we headed for the door. Outside was complete chaos. I grabbed the valet attendant as he hustled by and asked him what went on across the street. His answer was that someone was shot.

"Shot," Diamond asked and grabbed ahold of my arm. "Are they dead?"

"It looks like he's still alive," the valet replied and pointed.

Our eyes followed to where the EMT was successfully pulling the victim from the car. My Porsche was pulling up at that exact moment, which gave us a better view of the victim as they loaded him in the ambulance. Diamond noticed him first.

"Raheem," she screamed.

* * * * *

(Gloria)

Raheem supporters occupied the whole emergency waiting room at Shock Trauma. Besides me, Big Ma, Diamond, Prince, Pia, Quita, and a whole gang of thugs showed up. One of them even had the good sense to track down my sister and bring her to see about her son.

At the moment, we didn't really know what was up. All I had been able to get out of the nurse was that he had been shot up pretty bad. He was now in surgery and we were told to wait for doctors to find out more. I wanted to no more now. My lawyer instincts kicked in and I searched the room for Prince to see what he knew. He was huddled in a corner holding court with another dude. I headed over.

"All I know is someone gonna die tonight. Just give me a name and it's handled," I overheard a dude say when I walked up.

"Ma, this is Murder, Rah's main man," Prince introduced the speaker.

I nodded and asked Prince who first called with the info that Rah was shot. Before he could answer, Murder's phone rang and he stepped off.

"The girl Diamond called me Ma," was his reply.

I repeated her name and glanced in her direction. She was crying her eyes out over near Big Ma. Before I could fire off another question, Murder intervened.

"Yo, that was Moneybags on the horn. Yo said that he might be able to shed some light on the situation. I'm going outside to wait for him."

He headed for the exit while I and Prince headed in Diamond's locale. Shorty was really putting on a show; crying, hollering and carrying on. Even if Big Ma knew of her betrayal, she didn't let on by the way she was consoling the girl. Prince cleared his throat to get her attention and asked her to holler at him. Of course I followed. Once we were alone, Prince asked her what she knew about the shooting.

"I really don't know much. I was downtown at Rizzo's eating when I noticed police and the ambulance outside. As we were leaving, I got a good look at Rah as they were loading him the ambulance. That's when I called you," she said looking at Prince.

I knew the restaurant. It was the same joint that I had broken it off with Darius. The question was why was Rah there? Was he meeting Diamond or was he on some stalker shit?

"Who were you there with," I blurted out to her.

I could tell that she was pissed with me by the evil eye that she shot my way. She asked what that had to do with Rah getting shot. I rolled my eyes ready to get in her shit, but the voice of the doctor asking for Rah's relatives got my attention.

"I'm..." I started.

"I'm his mother," my sister Toria said cutting me off. We gave each other a look and I backed down. The doctor glanced at us both and then cleared his throat.

"I'm his grandmother," Big Ma inserted while giving us both an eye to let us know that now wasn't the time for our bickering. "You can speak in front of all of us."

Fresh

"Very well; the surgery was successful. He's stable now, but we're gonna list him as critical. We were able to remove the bullet out of his jaw, the one in his right shoulder and the one in his right arm. However, the bullet in his back is too dangerous to remove right now. It's too close to the spine. We're hoping it will move itself so we'll have a better chance of removing it in time. As it stands right now, Mr. Phillips has lost the use of his legs…"

"Oh my God, not my baby," Toria shouted as Big Ma grabbed her to make sure she didn't fall. I was busy trying to digest the paralyzed part. The doctor showed concern for Toria. A man in a suit pushed his way up front.

"Excuse me, I'm Detective Sheridan with the BDP and this is agent Cartagena." They flashed their badges. "I'll be investigating this matter. We need to know exactly when we'll be able to interrogate the victim."

They were clearly talking to the doctor, but I cut him off before he could respond. Had it just been a BDP investigator my red flag wouldn't have raised. The agent and his attendant bothered me. I whipped out my business card and introduced myself as Rah's attorney. My next question was for the agent. I asked her what she had to do with the case. They gave each other a look before Sheridan spoke.

"Agent Cartagena is assisting me with another matter and just decided to tag along. This is purely a BDP investigation."

They weren't fooling me. Something was definitely up and I think I had an idea what it was. I asked the agent for what branch did she work. When she replied that she was DEA, I had my answer. Shorty wasn't just tagging along. She was probably there to see what was up with her investigation of Raheem.

* * * * *

(Prince)

"Damn, bruh took four joints. He's paralyzed," Murder asked as he tried to pass me a lit cigarette.

Hearing that cuzzo was fucked up like that was fucking with me. I had slid out of the hospital as Ma started to give those jakes a hard time. Murder was still out front waiting on Bags so I joined him. He didn't have any weed so I made do with a cigarette until Bag's Lincoln MKS came creeping up. We hopped in and he pulled off.

"How the fuck is he," were the first words out of Bag's mouth. "Is he gonna make it?"

I gave him the rundown on Rah's situation; told him that he was fucked up pretty bad, but at least he was still living. I asked what kind of light he could shed on the situation after he digested

Rah's predicament. He nodded towards his front seat passenger.

"This is my little man Tiny right here. He was with Rah tonight."

Tiny turned around in his seat and handed me a blunt to spark before getting down to business. He told us that he and Rah were out plotting on yo. I cut him off right there. I wasn't in the mood to decipher a lot of yo's tonight. I needed him to speak in English so I could understand.

"We were plotting on the nigga T.O. Rah gave me the hit a few weeks ago. Anyway, T.O. was there with shorty and..."

I wasn't listening from that point on. All this boiled down to T.O. and that damned Diamond. I knew cuzzo was in his feelings over the situation, but had no idea that he had put a hit out on yo behind the shit.

Tiny ended up giving us the whole rundown; explained that he was down the block when shit went down. He said he didn't see shit. He didn't even hear a gunshot. He stated that if it wasn't for the window shattering and alerting the valet, Rah probably would have died out there.

I was pissed and ready for action after he finished. Cuzzo was out for the count and somebody needed to step up. The problem was that I didn't want to reveal my position by doing so. I knew Murder from the neighborhood personally. He was a stand up dude and probably could be trusted. My phone vibrated. It was my mother asking where I had disappeared to. I told her that I was in the parking lot and she told me to stay put. As soon as I hung up, Tiny spoke.

"I'm handling that nigga T.O. tonight. I don't give a fuck if I have to knock on that nigga door to do it."

I didn't encourage nor try to stop him. Something was telling me that T.O. was behind all of this. Shit could only get better with him out of the way. I turned to Murder.

"You are Rah's second in command. I'm sure I can trust you to keep everything in line in the streets," I questioned and he answered with a nod.

I saw my mother approaching, switched phone into with Murder and made my way to her direction. Of course she was on the phone when I approached. She hung up and cursed out loud.

"That was your sister. She got her phone off tonight of all nights."

I stated that Princess was alright where she was and told her that I had just learned about Rah's hit on T.O. Her response was did I think it was him. I told her that was all we had to go on for now. She thought about that and finally nodded.

"I think that all the drug dealings should cease as of today. One of those police was a fucking DEA agent. I'm willing to bet my fucking paycheck that she is here to investigate your cousin. I hope that you have been taking my advice and distancing yourself from the street action," She warned.

* * * * *

(Princess)

I woke up alone in Fire's guest bedroom. After shaking the cobwebs from my head, I checked the clock. It was after two. I smiled as thoughts of last night flooded my memory.

After his recording session, we ended up having a late dinner prepared by his chef. I retired to the room to bathe and ended up falling asleep. Fire crept in claiming that he couldn't sleep. If he thought he was fucking, he was sadly mistaken. To my surprise, he took a seat on the edge of the bed and we ended up talking until the wee hours of the morning.

I got up to go take care of my morning hygiene. It was on the restroom mirror that I found a note explaining that he was waiting for me by his pool. I found him almost thirty minutes later in his mixing room doing some last minute adjustments to Jada's song.

Before I could make my presence known, his phone rang. He answered and started speaking in rapid Spanish. Seeing his phone made me realize that I had left mines upstairs. Before I could make an about face, he slung his phone into the wall and got to his feet.

"Fucking bitch," he shouted.

"What's wrong," I inquired, while noting that temper tantrums were in his life.

He gave me a look, started to comment and evidently changed his mind. Yo switched up and put a smile on his face; asked if I had eaten anything yet. I let him know that his maid was preparing me a sandwich. He nodded before looking at his watch.

"We got an appointment to make. You gonna have to take that sandwich to go," he stated while grabbing my hand and leading me to the kitchen.

"Appointment; what…"

"Never mind all that. You just relax and let me make up for not picking you up from the airport personally," he said before speaking rapidly to his maid in Spanish.

She busied herself with my sandwich while I took personal inventory of what I was wearing. Luckily I had taken the time to get cute. I still didn't know if the J Brand jeans and corset that I was wearing was appropriate for what he had in mind. I asked him if I was dressed okay. He took a quick look, kissed his fingers and told me that I looked marvelous.

Fresh

The next thing I knew, he had grabbed my food and ushered me through a door to his six car garage. Inside, besides his impressive fleet of cars he had a Yamaha bike, a chopper motorcycle, two dirt bikes, and three four wheelers. We made our way over to his Maserati coupe. He asked if I could drive stick. I gave him a sarcastic look.

"Is Barack Obama our president?"

He smiled and tossed me the keys. Twenty minutes later, we were pulling up to Hartsfield airport. Again I asked him where we were going. He ignored me and directed me towards the runway where a private G5 and pilot were waiting for our arrival. Once we were aboard and airborne, Fire lit up a blunt and poured us each a glass of champagne.

"To the pleasures of flying first class," he toasted with a smirk.

I clinked glasses with him; told him that I didn't appreciate him whisking me away like this; especially dressed the way that I was. He waved off my outfit and told me that I was in good hands with him. I commented that he was trying to impress. He asked me was I in fact impressed. I blushed and finally nodded. He passed me the blunt.

"Well, I'm on my job then," he replied.

* * * * *

(T.O.)

"Well, I guess I'll see you when you get here then. And drive safely, baby girl," I warned before hanging up.

I was with Bruh in route to my farm house in West Virginia. After Diamond climbed into that ambulance with that nigga last night, I had to get on my phone to report to Bonnie that her hit was unsuccessful.

She was disappointed and explained how she had watched old boy's crib and was ready to call it a night when he suddenly came out to his whip. She said that she followed him downtown and watched him get into that nondescript car. She said that she decided right then to end things.

It was Bruh who put two and two together about the reason yo was at the exact same restaurant that I and shorty were eating at. After a little prodding, I made a call down to the BDP and found out that Rah was strapped up like the Taliban in that car. Evidently, he was trying to put my career on hold with the shit that he had with him.

With that said, I knew I had beef. My problem was that I didn't know who else was after me. True, yo was on the scene of the crime, but I also knew that he had enough sense to have some shooters on the job. Bruh agreed with me and suggested that I retire to my farm house for a few days while he put his ear to the streets to figure things out.

I agreed with him, but I had my own plans. I got my nigga Baby Ray out of D.C. to loan me a team of goons and instantly put the full court press down in the hood. I told Bonnie to forget about Rah for the moment and to get on that Prince situation. I might as well hit them hard to show my dominance.

With those moves in place, I contacted my one and only daughter, Natasha, and asked her to join me up at the ranch. Shorty was schooling down south at N.C. State, trying to become an engineer. We barely see each other, so I figured that now would be the perfect opportunity to get some quality time in.

* * * * *

(Prince)

Intensive care visiting hours are tricky. The hospital was on some fifteen minute visit every two hour shit. I made it my business to be in that room for my cousin every visit though. On this particular visit, we were alone though.

I glanced at my cousin and shook my head. Motherfuckers had really done a job on my nigga. Yo didn't even look like himself. It seemed like he had lost twenty pounds over night or something. His face was bandaged up like a mummy due to the bullet in the jaw. The doctor did say that he would talk again so that was a good thing. I reached for his hand.

"Everything gonna be alright my nigga. This ain't as bad as it seems. You wake up and we gonna get you the best doctors that money can buy. The doctors have already given us some doctors that could probably pull that surgery off. Shit, we get you that treatment and you'll be back on your feet in no time.

In the meantime, I've decided to shut shop down. Moneybags and the boy Murder claim that they gonna ride for you. I want to put in some work myself. You're like my brother. Nigga fuck with you and they got to see me. Real talk; I just wish I knew who did this sit to you and things will be a lot easier. I mean…I got ideas, but I'm not sure. Who the fuck did you let get this close to you cuzzo," I asked out loud, getting a little frustrated.

I was talking to myself but Rah must have heard me. I felt a squeeze or tug on my hand. His eyes fluttered but remained closed. I looked towards the door trying to decide whether I should call a nurse. Before I could decide, he opened his eyes and licked his lips.

"It was a white bitch bruh. Some white bitch…" he mumbled before closing his eyes again.

* * * * *

(Princess)

My surprise turned out to be a trip to MIA. A limo whisked us to the Fountain Blue Hotel, where Fire had arranged front row seats to a Prada fashion show. I was both amazed and a little envious of the beautiful models that strutted up and down the runway.

After the show was over, Fire produced backstage passes. We walked up to an attractive lady smoking a cigarillo, while issuing orders to an assistant. Her face lit up when she noticed Fire standing near her. She instantly held her arms open.

"Bernard Vasquez Jr.; get your behind over here and give your auntie a hug."

Fire did as he was asked. After she released him, he turned to me and introduced the lady as his aunt Sade. Her attention was strictly on her nephew until she did glance my way. After getting a good look, she did a double take and reached for my hand.

"Ah, Bernie, you were right. She is a beauty and she's tall enough," she complimented while twirling me around like a ballerina. "She has an ass, but hey, ass is in these days. Are you signed to anyone?"

My voice was caught in my throat. Fire was wooing the hell out of a bitch. I had only mentioned to him last night that my dread was to become a runway model and here he was introducing me to someone in the business. I heard myself mumbling out the name of my agency. She frowned as if I had been had. Fire spoke up.

"My aunt is vice president of Show Me Modeling. These are her girls who just put on the show."

His aunt produced a card from thin air. She asked if I had a portfolio with me. Fire stepped in again and told her that this trip was a surprise and that I had come unprepared. An assistant rushed up and cut off her reply. After listening to what her employee had to say, she turned to us and announced that she had to run, but would surely see us at the after party tonight.

She skated off and I turned to Fire and immediately jumped into his arms. We hadn't checked in yet so after getting that done, we headed up to our room. When we finally made it to our door, I had a thought.

"Your aunt just mentioned an after party. I can't go to a party dressed like this. I told you..."

He cut me off with a finger to my lips and then opened our room door. Evidently, he had this planned in advance because right there in the front room of our suite were racks and racks of clothes. I saw over twenty boxes of shoes. Before I even got close, I noticed the logo and knew that this was all Prada. I tuned to Fire who had a smirk on his face.

"Chill ma, I told you that you're with me."

My pussy got wet instantly. I got an idea; approached him slowly and offered my tongue while gently releasing his belt buckle. It was time to reward him properly.

Chapter 15

(Prince)

"Mommy, can I kiss daddy before we leave like I used to," my daughter asked.

My eyes were closed but I was fully awake. I was just resting up a bit, enjoying the feel and smell of my old bed. Pia felt sorry for a nigga last night after she came through to visit Rah. I hadn't left the hospital since he had been admitted earlier in the week.

His condition had been upgraded from critical to stable. He was now awake and fully conscious. Right now and until the bullet that was lodged in his spine was removed, he has no use of his legs. The operation that they offered is tricky and if something should go wrong, he could lose the movement in the rest of his body. However, if the surgery is successful, he could regain his strength and walk again. The decision is to be made by Rah and Rah only.

Anyway, Pia rescued a nigga last night when she visited. After giving me a hug for support, she sniffed my underarm and commented that I was a little tart. Before I could reply, it dawned on her that I hadn't left the hospital in the last couple of days and had been surviving off bird baths in the hospital restrooms. She instantly took control by grabbing my coat and ushering me towards the exit. Once in her car, she announced that she was taking me to her house for a shower and a little rest and relaxation. I didn't argue.

"Yes baby, you can kiss him but be careful not to wake him," Pia warned Asia.

It wasn't until after my kiss and I heard the front door click that I opened my eyes. After m restroom break, I searched the dresser for boxers and hit the jackpot. A look in the closet produced about six outfits that I suspected she had picked up from the cleaners with her shit. I ran into my first obstacle when I noticed that my toothbrush was missing in the restroom. I brushed that off and just used hers while in route downstairs to cook me something. My cell chimed when I reached the kitchen and stopped me in my tracks.

"Who the fuck," I asked before answering. The caller ID stated that the call was from Petersburg, Virginia, but it wasn't the same number that usually showed up when my father called me.

"Hello?"

"Son, this is your father. Something strange has happened and I don't want to explain it right now. I need for you to come to the prison right now and pick me up."

My heart almost skipped a beat. I could tell from the tone of his voice that he was either in the room with crackers or he was worried that someone was listening on a bug. I decided to play along.

"Pick you up?"

"That's right son; come pick your old man up." I could hear the smile in his voice. "My lawyer petitioned the President for a pardon a couple of months ago and they just informed me that it was granted. They are releasing me this morning. I can leave just as soon as you get here to pick me up. Now please, don't waste another second and come get me."

I hung up and started to get dressed. The day had finally arrived and I was moving as if I was traumatized. My feelings were mixed. I was just a pee wee when my father was arrested. For some reason, I felt like my life was about to change drastically.

* * * * *

(T.O.)

"Are you sure that you can't stay just one more day; just until the weekend at least," I asked my daughter as I loaded her luggage into her Infiniti.

"I wish I could daddy, but I got a paper that is due Monday; plus its Jeff's birthday..." she answered while leaning in for a farewell kiss.

Fresh

I sighed out loud. Jeff was a knucklehead that she was dating. I had a feeling that the paper she was speaking of was a front and this Jeff character was the real reason she was rushing back. I had never met the dude personally, but made a mental note to get a check on his ass.

I ended up giving her the kiss she requested and watched as her car disappeared up the driveway. My little girl was all grown up. My live in housekeeper met me at the door.

"Can I make you breakfast this morning? Maybe grits and eggs will make you feel better," the old Hispanic lady asked.

I agreed and headed to my office. After flicking on ESPN, I dialed Diamond's number and got her voicemail. That pissed me off so I dialed another number.

Bruh was coming down later to update me on the happenings in the city. Word from his last visit was that it was damn near impossible for Bonnie to get to either Rah or Prince. He said that Rah had two officers guarding his room waiting to charge him with a gun charge. As for Prince, the reason she couldn't get to him was because he hadn't left the fucking hospital.

As for the streets, we were winning that war. Bruh reported that our sneak attack was a success and had shut down both of Rah's spots as planned. None of his lieutenants were harmed, but seven soldiers and two innocent bystanders felt our wrath. Our message was loud and clear, because his shops hadn't attempted to reopen.

Business was also starting to pick up. Two of my old customers who Rah had stolen were back calling. That was a good thing. Hopefully, other niggas would start to fall back in line.

A sexy voice came over the line and reminded me that I had just dialed a number. Her name was Chyna Doll and she was a stripper at my club. A nigga needed some pussy to get my mind off things and I was sure that hers could do the trick.

* * * * *

(Princess)

"Dr. Robbins please dial 1417...repeat, Dr. Robbins, please dial 1417."

The voice over the loud speaker woke me from my slumber. I wiped saliva from my chin as I looked around my surroundings. Big Ma was to my right. Diamond was nowhere in sight. My aunt Toria wasn't present either.

I checked my phone for messages. No calls or texts had been received. That pissed me off. The nigga Fire was definitely on some shit. After the after party the other night, we definitely got down and dirty. I had his ass speaking in tongues, and the whole nine. His dick game was like that too. That aside, once I found we made it back to Atlanta and I retrieved my absentee phone, I found out about Rah and what happened. Of course, I boarded the first thing smoking and the rest is history. That was four days ago. I hadn't heard from his ass yet.

The nigga had me all out of character and questioning myself. Did he take me for a jump-off? Was the pussy not good to him? Did I get too freaky too quick? Nevertheless, the nigga definitely had his people fucked up. It's not even in my character to sweat a nigga. And looking at shit from another perspective, so what, I gave up the pussy. The nigga paid dearly for it.

I laughed out loud and scrolled through my phone until Hood's' name showed up. It was too early to be calling him so I simply left a message that I was missing his ass and for him to call me. To my surprise, my phone rang in my hand and it was him.

"Damn, baby girl, I've been missing you too. Where in the fuck have you been?"

I smiled. He had been hitting my phone these last few days but I had been caught up with everything that I had going on and told him.

"Damn, that's some fucked up shit. I hate to hear that Rah got hit up like that. Yo's an alright dude."

I agreed that my cousin was one of a kind then scolded him for speaking of him in the past tense. I let him know that Rah was alive and kicking and explained that my people were looking into some doctors to get him back on his feet.

"That's what's good. So...when do you think he's gonna be ready for business or do you think it's too soon..." he asked.

I shook my head. I had just explained that my cuzzo was damn near on his death bed and here this nigga was wondering about some fucking drugs.

"I really don't know what's up with all that right now," I lied in a sarcastic tone. I still had access to the work, but was under strict orders not to touch anything.

"Well, that's what's good then. I'll just have to go another route then." He hesitated and then continued. "I miss you though ma. When can I come and check you out.

I told him that anytime was good and suggested as fast he could make it. He told me that he would hit the highway just as soon as could get in touch with his driver. I checked my watch after hanging up with him. I had just enough time to brush the sleep off my breath before the a.m. visit.

Diamond was waking Big Ma up when I came out the restroom. I rolled my eyes at the bitch; was really tired of looking at her ass. The only reason I hadn't confronted the bitch about the whole T.O. situation was because she stayed under Big

Fresh

Ma. You thought that she was slick but I was on to her. She refused to go inside and visit Rah, claiming that she didn't want to see him in that condition, but I knew the truth. Shorty was just scared that Rah was gonna reject that ass.

* * * * *

(Prince)

I made it to Petersburg in record time. Pop's paperwork was in order and he was ready to go. I caught up with everything that was going on with the family on the highway. When we made it to the Potomac Mills exit, he pointed for me to take it.

"Do you have any money on you," he asked as we made our way into the wall.

I only had a few hundred, but told him not to worry and produced one of my credit cards. Ma had court today so we took our time shopping. We hit up Nordstrom and had a ball. Pops was feeling the preppy look; said that he wanted to go straight causal. I convinced him to grab a few pairs of Armani jeans to go with those V-neck sweaters and suede blazers that he was picking out. After we got him fresh, he wanted to go pick out some jewelry. I pointed him in the direction of the Cartier store.

After checking out the price on some of the items he asked what my limit on the cards were. That was the trick question because I wasn't even sure. The card in particular was my company card that I used strictly for construction supplies and whatnot. We ended up putting the fucker to the test anyway and it stood up. The first item that caught his eye was a seven carat flawless princess cut engagement ring with an extra three carats surrounding the band.

"Do you think that she will say yes," he asked.

I whistled and admired the ring. I had no doubt in my mind that mom was gonna accept his proposal and told him so. He examined the piece again as if second guessing the size. He actually wanted to upgrade, but I convinced him that it was good. With that settled, he asked me what my sister's taste was. I pointed out a simple platinum necklace with an iced out heart pendant for Princess and a couple of gold bangles for Asia.

"I know my daughter. This won't do," he said while shaking his head. "She gonna awful jealous after she sees this ring I have for her mother.

I thought about what he said and agreed that he had a point. We ended up trading the necklace in for a diamond choker. It was damn near three o'clock when we made it out of the mall.

"Where to now, B-more," I asked as I crank up.

He wanted to know what time my mother usually made it out of court. I told him that we made good timing because she usually went to check for Rah when she got off.

"That's perfect timing then. Swing by a grocery store or something. I want to cook for everybody tonight," he said while reaching for my phone. "In the meantime, you can tell me how to get your sister on this thing.

* * * * *

(Princess)

A blue Audi Quattro was parked beside my Lexus when I made it home that evening. It wasn't until I stepped out of my Bentley that I noticed Hood and a senior citizen sitting in the whip. Hood instantly rolled down his window and whistled at my car.

"So you're doing it like this in B-more now. You must think that one of these grimy ass niggas won't snatch your pretty ass out of that motherfucker," he joked, as he got out and gave me a hug.

"How long have you been waiting here?"

"Too motherfucking long, which is why I think it's about time that you gave me a house key. Waiting out here ain't even cool, especially with my situation," he said.

I mumbled something about him not paying any bills as we made our way to the elevator. Of course he offered to handle all my bills, but I let that shit roll off my shoulder. There wasn't no way any nigga was getting keys to this castle besides Prince. He was persistent thought.

"Oh, I'm not good enough to have a key to the crib. And here I thought we were exclusive. You got me fucked up."

I stopped in my tracks before placing my key in my door. I asked him since when did we become exclusive. He started to stutter.

"I'm saying, I know how you feel about a nigga and those streets. I'm moving real slow now. I got the city on smash with this shit that you're providing." He smiled that killer smile of his. "I'm getting lonely down that motherfucker. So I thought that you may want to come down and keep me company permanently."

I studied him, decided that he was serious and stepped into my house. Yo is truly one on my weaknesses. A life down south with him was real tempting. I had already visited Durham a couple of times. It wasn't Baltimore but I could adjust. Hood pulled me down on the couch beside him and asked me what I thought about his question. This time, it was me who stuttered.

"I mean…it sounds tempting, but…"

"But what," he prodded.

I had to think fast. My club came to mind. He waved that off and told me that he would sponsor another club and I could even keep the one in D.C. He even mentioned helping me out. I raised an eyebrow at him.

"What? I told you that I'm bored down there."

I started to reply but he stopped me; told me to take my time to decide. He reminded me that Durham or he wasn't going anywhere. He did tell me not to take forever with my answer though. I agreed with him and then headed to my room. I hadn't had a shower since yesterday and I knew my pussy was in desperate need of some attention. My phone vibrated as I turned to the shower. It was Prince.

"What do you want, ugly," I teased.

"Ugly?"

"Who is ..." I started before catching on to the voice. "Hey Daddy!"

Hood came into the restroom and smacked me across the ass. He gave me a look and licked his lips. I motioned at the phone and mouthed that my dad was on the line.

"Hey, beautiful, I have a surprise for you."

Ooh, a surprise; I love surprises. What you got?"

"You're gonna have to come get it."

"Come get it," I asked before it dawned on me. I screamed at the top of my lungs.

Hood looked at me like I was crazy. I asked where he was. He told me that he was pulling into the Safeway over on Boston Street. I told him that I was about five minutes from him and he was not to move until I made it there.

Of course Hood was in my shit for an explanation. I gave him the short version as I headed towards the door; said some shit about my mom putting in for a pardon and that the President must've came through. I ended up telling him to chill and that I wouldn't be long.

The only thing I hated most about living so close to downtown was the midday work traffic. My five minute trip was sure to turn into maybe fifteen with this traffic. My phone vibrated and took me out my thoughts.

"I'm coming right now. I'm in traffic…" I started without even looking at my caller ID.

"You're in Atlanta?"

The voice belonged to Fire. I got even more excited and put on my sweetest voice; started explaining that I was in Baltimore but thought that he was my worrisome ass brother calling. Then I dropped my sweet voice.

"Lord, listen to me explaining when I should be cursing your ass out," I said.

"Curse me out?"

"Yeah, cursing your ass out. What type of fowl shit are you into. It's been days and you haven't even called to check on me."

Fresh

I got even madder when he had the nerve to burst out laughing. He started mocking my voice; said that he loved my accent. I pulled into the store parking lot and hopped out.

"Listen at you, what's so fucking funny," I asked.

"I know it's not funny and I apologize. It's just…"

I made it to the store. They weren't in the checkout lines. I headed for the fruit department and started checking every aisle.

"You apologize? Is that it," I asked as I started with aisle 18.

"Yeah, I apologize. I mean, I knew that you were busy with your family situation. I did dial your number like twice but got the voicemail both times. Shit, I've been busy my damn self while you're bullshitting." He let his words trail off.

I was so busy inspecting the aisles while trying to listen to him that I bumped into an old lady. I cursed out loud and started apologizing. She accepted and moved on. I took a deep breath and tried to get my shit together.

"Are you okay," Fire asked.

"I'm good," I responded and then went on to say that I was looking for my pops at the moment. "Can I call you back?"

He told me that he wanted to run something by me before we got off the phone. He said that he had business in Philly to tend to, but wanted to come early so he could come check me out. He said that he would understand if I couldn't, with everything that I had going on.

"Nah, you're good. Text your flight info and I'll pick you up from the airport."

He told me that he would do just that and I hung up. I was feeling even happier that I was a second ago. Someone calling my name got my attention. I took off running towards my pops like a kid on Christmas morning.

* * * * *

(Gloria)

"How did it go in court today Ms. Phillips," my secretary asked as soon as I made it into my office.

I told her that I would find out soon and headed straight for my office. She was right behind me running down a string of must dos. I headed for my bar and poured myself a stiff one. A drink and a cigarette were in order. She finished up her list and pointed to a package that my private investigator had left. I dismissed her for the day.

After she was gone, I sat behind my desk and picked up the package. It was info on King's friend that he asked for. I scanned it real quick and tossed it in my briefcase.

Fresh

Everything was quiet at the hospital. The doctor ended up extending Rah's stay in ICU for one more day. He didn't give any specific reasons why; just said that it wouldn't hurt. Big Ma had left to attend church. That left Diamond and Toria there. I asked my sister had my children been there that evening.

"I haven't seen Prince all day. Princess was here earlier and said that she was going home to shower," she said while yawning. "I guess that shower got good to her. Anyway, I'm hungry and I need a pack of cigarettes."

Even though I didn't like her ass, she was my sister. Plus I was proud of the way that she had stepped up in her son's time of need. I dug through my purse, gave her ten dollars and then dialed my daughter's number.

"Hey ma, where are you at?"

I looked at the phone to see if I had dialed the right number. Rarely did Princess use this tone. I told her that I was good and then asked where she was.

"I'm um...I'm out to your house."

"My house," I asked and then heard Prince laugh in the background. "Is that your brother that I hear?"

She confirmed that it was. I relaxed a bit. Her presence at my house was a total surprise.

Prince still considered my house his though. I asked her why my house was the sudden hangout.

"Oh, we got hungry. There wasn't anything at my house so we decided to raid your fridge. And by the way, we're cooking so feel free to join us."

I told them that I would do just that and left the hospital. Both of their coupes were kissing when I pulled up. Pia's wagon was parked out front also. I smelled seafood as I entered my crib. I made my way towards the kitchen.

"Smells good in here; what exactly are y'all cooking," I asked as I walked inside.

The room became quiet. They hadn't heard me enter. Finally I heard a familiar voice come out of the little restroom that I had attached to my kitchen.

"We're having filet mignon with a side of creole jambalaya. I got some broccoli and brown rice to finish it off. For dessert, Miss Asia helped me whip up a pound cake," King informed.

I almost wanted to faint. I don't know how I ended up in his arms. Maybe I floated. Our first kiss was so passionate. Afterwards, I pushed him back to get a better view at him. My hands searched his body as if looking for gunshot wounds. I needed to feel him to make sure that this wasn't a dream. He picked me up and spun me around.

I was speechless once he put me down; had so much to say. I glanced around the room.

Fresh

Everyone had a smile on their face. They had tricked me. I felt like cursing but I didn't. When I finally did open my mouth to say something, King put a finger to my lips and bent to one knee.

"Before you say anything, I need to know if you'll be my wife," he asked as he pulled a box from his pocket. "Gloria Denise Phillips; the mother of my two kids; will you be more that my baby's mother. Be my wife."

I looked down at the sparkling rock that winked at me. Everyone in the room gasped at the diamond's brilliance. Even though this was an instant important moment of my life, my mind still did an appraisal of the product. The ring was flawless no doubt. It probably set him back over a hundred. It was magnificent. I almost shivered with delight. Bug Ma, who I hadn't even noticed sitting over near the bar, got my attention.

"Child, don't just stand there. Answer the man so we can eat."

The room burst out laughing. King was still on his knees. I stuck out my finger. The ring fit perfectly. I pulled him up into my arms.

"Yes," was all I could muster up.

Chapter 16

(Princess)

Hood shook me awake with a paranoid look on his face. He told me that someone was at the door and asked me if I was expecting anyone. I mumbled that I wasn't and rolled back over. I had only just gotten in the house a couple of hours ago. My pop's dinner had run into the wee hours. Then Hood wanted some time when I came home. Shit, a bitch was exhausted.

"This shit ain't working. Every time I come to this motherfucker you either got a house full or somebody knocking. What the fuck do you have a doorman for anyway? I thought they were supposed to screen visitors…"

His aggravation woke me up. I slid into a rove. He was busy putting on his clothes. Whoever was knocking was surely pissed. I snatched the door open without even asking who it was and got the surprise of my life.

"I see how you treat me. Let me find out that this is payback for not picking you up in Atlanta," Fire asked with a scowl on his face.

I put my hands over my mouth. Throughout all of the excitement that I had going on, I had totally forgot about him arriving this morning. Fire took my gesture as an invitation to come in. He grabbed his Vuitton carry all and rolled it pass me. I shut the front door and leaned against.it.

"I'm so, so, sooooo sorry Fire. My ...my father is home. We had this big dinner last night. I don't even know what to say."

His phone rang and interrupted my plea. He glanced at the screen and held up a finger. He told his caller that he was god and had got a cab. He sat down on my cough; the same couch that Hood had fucked me on last night. My Seven jeans and Hood's True Religions were there for evidence. I grabbed those and started to tidy up. I took the item and tossed them into Prince's room.

Fire's eyes were on me. I heard something fall in my room; sounded like perfume from my dresser. Fire heard it too. He gave me a look as if asking did I have company. I bit my lip for confirmation. He stood.

"Ain't this some shit. I come all the way..." He stopped whatever he was gonna say and brushed past me. I followed him out into the hallway.

"Fire, I'm sorry. Let me explain."

"Don't trip Princess. I should've known that you..." He stopped at the elevator. "What is really fucked up is that you knew I was coming and you still had a nigga over. What type of shit is that?"

I didn't have an answer. What he said was true. I knew he was thinking that I was the biggest slut in the world right now and I couldn't even dispute it. The elevator buzzed and he stepped into it. I didn't even try to stop him.

When I made it back into my crib, Hood was sitting on the couch whispering into his phone. I heard him ordering his driver to come get him. For some reason, I was glad that he was leaving. His gun was in his lap. It was obvious that he was pissed.

I walked right passed him and into my bedroom and started brushing my teeth. Getting caught up like this was so unfamiliar to me. I felt so uncomfortable right now. When he came into the room, I asked him casually if he was about to get missing.

"Yeah, it's getting crowded in here. I think that I better make myself scarce before I get myself into trouble," he grunted.

I ignored his comment and hopped into the shower. I wanted to scream. I mean, Hood is my beau and all. I really didn't want to hurt him, but right now, I was feeling some type of way about Fire. Plus, Hood had issues. The nigga was on the run for Christ's sake. He was unstable and unpredictable.

Now Fire was...Fire was new and exciting; successful, rich and spontaneous. His future was bright. He had connections in high places. Hands down, he was definitely a good catch.

When I stepped out the shower, my house was quiet. I did a quick walk through. Hood was definitely gone. I locked my doors and headed for my phone. Fire answered on the third ring.

"Fire, please don't hang up. I have something I want to tell you…" I started.

* * * * *

(Gloria)

King was at the kitchen table sipping coffee while looking through the file I had left for him when I came in from my morning jog. In front of him were the remains of the breakfast I had fixed for him. I went over and planted a kiss on his neck.

"I can't believe that you had enough energy to jog this morning after the night we had," he commented.

I gave a naughty snicker; told him that I had to keep in shape for his attention. The wall clock said that I was late for work. I headed up the stairs. No matter what, the show must go on. Shit, I couldn't skip work even if I wanted to. I was in the middle of a jury selection.

While in the shower, I planned my day. I needed to inform my partners of the immediate vacation time I was about to take. I had to tie up all work related issues. I reminded myself to reserve the private jet that I was chartering. I didn't know how long court would take, but I had plans to fly out as soon as the jury was finished.

King's nose was still in that file when I returned back downstairs. I poured myself a cup of coffee to go and sat down across from him.

"What are your plans for today," I asked.

He set his paper down and stretched; said that he wanted to do some more shopping and would probably hook up with Prince to see if they could find his old friend. He pointed to the file.

I pointed at the papers as well and asked him what was up with the dude anyway. I admitted that he looked familiar but I couldn't quite place him.

Bruh is good people. I used to run with him back in the day. I really just want to hook up and reminisce," he offered.

I waved a warning finger at his ass. I knew this man and common sense told me that he was up to something.

"This isn't the eighties anymore King. Don't come home on that boss shit. Remember that things have changed. And please don't forget the promise you made to me either."

He leaned over for a kiss and told me to calm my nerves. He said that he knew what year it was and that he was very aware. He pulled me onto his lap and asked me had he told me that he loved me that morning. I scooted out of his lap before he started something.

"No you haven't, but you'll have plenty of time to tell me later."

I headed over to the cabinet and retrieved the I-phone that I had copped for him a couple of weeks ago. After turning it on, I gave him a brief rundown on how it worked.

"This thing has a navigational system and all. Technology is a mother," he stated while flipping through the instruction manual.

I tossed him a set of keys to everything that I owned. I told him that he could find the remote to the garage in the Benz. I started to tell him exactly how shit worked but he cut me off.

"I already about know, and if I don't I'll teach myself," he said with a grin. "You'll be surprised at how much shit I read up on while in there. Believe it or not, I always knew that I was coming home one day."

I had to nod. No matter how many rejections we faced, King always kept a positive outlook on things. I reached into my purse and slid an envelope across the table to him.

"Here's some pocket change and a few credit cards. Treat yourself today honey. Don't go buying everybody else gifts and shit," I told him.

He snatched up the envelope and did a quick inventory of the ten grand that I had inside and then promptly told me that he had everything under control.

* * * * *

(Prince)

"So, when do I get to meet the big man," Quita asked.

I was dressing, getting ready to meet my pops over on the west side. He was coming from Columbia, which gave me enough time to swing by the hospital to see about Rah. I told her that I didn't know what he had planned but if she would just call me later, I would swing through.

She climbed out of bed in her birthday suit. Shorty was gorgeous, even with her little plump belly. She started to mumble something under her breath. I grabbed her and asked her what was wrong, even though I already had an idea.

"It's...my...fucking...birthday nigga," she yelled with conviction. She had her hands on her waist and was rolling those pretty eyes too. "That's right, November 27 and your ass was about to..."

I turned my back and reached in my pocket. When I turned around with her thirty thousand dollar Frank Muller watch that she had been hinting at, she instantly shut the fuck up and started screaming.

"Yeah, now look at you; who's the man," I boasted. She jumped into my arms and started kissing me. That warm cat against my midsection was starting to arouse me. I pushed her away and told her to be ready later on because I had more for her.

I got out of there without having to sex shorty and decided to skip my visit with Rah. When I reached Big Ma's house, my pops was already there sitting outside on the porch. I got out of the car to join him. He commented on the weed as I took a seat next to him and started twisting up an el.

"Man, this is good weather," he observed while taking in the surroundings.

He pointed up the street and asked me if Mrs. Evelynn still stayed that way. I told him that she passed over five years ago and that shocked him. Mrs. Evelynn was a legend in the neighborhood.

He went into reminiscent mode for a minute and started pointing out old landmarks and the times that he had there. I listened and took everything in. For years, I had heard the rumors of how he had once controlled this whole city, but never heard it from him. We stayed out there until I finished my blunt before he asked if I had brought the utensils that he had asked for. We went and climbed into my Bentley. I reached under the seat and revealed two .38 revolvers. He took one and gave me an address out towards Cantonville.

Twenty minutes later we arrived at the destination. It was a modest little row house in a suburban neighborhood. Pops told me to circle the block once and then pointed to a phone booth. He stepped out and dialed a number. I took the time to call and check on Rah. When he stepped back into the car, he pointed up the block.

"Up the street in that diner parking lot is a white minivan with a white person behind the wheel." I looked in that direction subtly. "I don't know if the driver is male or female but I do know that they have been following us since we left your grandmother's house."

My first thoughts were what my mom had told me about the feds and Rah. My pops dismissed that one though and told me that it was only one person and the feds didn't work like that. Before I could come up with something else, he told me not to worry about it and directed me back to the previous address. I made it my business to ride pass the diner though.

"Do you recognize her," he asked once I pulled in front of the house.

I shook my head no. I wasn't too worried about the situation though. The person in the car back there was a bitch with shades on. She was on her cell phone and probably not thinking of us.

The door to the house swung open and a man stepped out onto the porch. We cuffed our guns before stepping out and heading up the walk. The man smiled brighter than the moon on a dark night. He looked familiar but I couldn't place him. Pops gave him a brotherly hug when we entered.

"God damn, King, it really is you isn't it," the man confirmed after shutting the door after us.

"You're damn right, it's me in the flesh," my pops teased before pointing at me. "And this is my son Prince. Prince, meet my good friend Bruh."

When I heard yo's name, instant recognition came into my mind. The dude that we were visiting was also a good friend of T.O.'s. I remembered him from the night we met at El Dorado's.

* * * * *

(Raheem)

There you are Mr. Phillips. How do you feel," the old nurse on duty asked me as she fluffed my pillows.

I grunted. They were finishing getting me settled into my own private room. The doctor had removed the feeding tube from my earlier and I could talk a little. My throat was still feeling like shit so I chose my words wisely.

She pointed out a few gadgets and explained how they worked before making her exit. As soon as she left, I picked up the phone and dialed Prince's number. His phone went straight to voicemail and that pissed me off. I wanted to holler at him about our operation and direct him on how to handle things. I knew the streets were probably starving without me and knowing Prince, he had probably shut down shop completely. I tried to think of Moneybags' number but my mom walked through the door and surprised me.

"Hey baby, how are you feeling today?"

I looked my mother up and down and admired how pretty she could be when she wasn't high. I told her that I was feeling alright and asked where Big Ma was.

"She's out in the hallway trying to convince Diamond to come in in see you."

Hearing Diamond's name shocked me. I didn't know if I was pissed that she was here or glad. I asked when she arrived.

"When did she arrive? Hell, that girl's been here with you since day one. She may leave once a day to shower, but other than that, she's been right out there with us. She was just scared to come inside and visit you," she added.

A knock came to the door. A dude and a female stuck their heads inside. I knew they were police instantly. The dude introduced himself as Detective Sheridan and the lady as Agent Cartagena. They said they wanted to ask me some questions about the shooting. Sheridan was doing all the talking but I kept my eyes on shorty.

"Mr. Phillips?" I snapped out of my trance. "I asked if you could tell us what went on the night of the shooting."

"Umm, I really don't remember much," I whispered. "Just some bum bitch asked me for a light and when I said that I didn't have one, she shot me."

Cartagena was taking notes. She immediately shut her notebook and gave Sheridan a glare. Evidently, she didn't believe me.

"That's it? She just shot you because you didn't have a light," Sheridan probed.

My mom cut in then and told them that they had heard me correctly. They ignored her and asked if I could identify the bum. I wasn't gonna give them a description though. Shit, I had already said too much by offering that it was a lady. They glanced at each other again.

"Were you at the restaurant alone that night Mr. Phillips?" This question came from the bitch.

"Listen, my sister who you all met before is his attorney. Maybe y'all should be asking her these questions. Hold on a sec…" my mom started.

They clammed up then and told my mother that my aunt wasn't needed for this meeting. My mom cut them off again and said that she thought my aunt would be needed. She instructed me not to say another word and then told the cops that I was exercising my right to remain silent. Both cops turned to look at me. I pulled the sheets up and yawned loudly. They got the message. The interview was over.

* * * * *

(Prince)

"And so your father says, 'I'm the boss. Now if you'll excuse me.'"

We were on our second drinks; had been listening to the old heads reminisce for the last thirty minutes. They talked about everything from old flings to police corruption.

"Yeah, those were some good times," Bruh stated as he looked at his watch. "Now that we are a little loose, maybe you should tell me how you got out and why I'm one of the first stops that you made upon your release."

My pops gave him a disappointed look and stated that he had known Bruh for thirty years and didn't think that he needed the questioning. When Bruh started to protest, my pops cut him off. He went into details of how he was released as far as the pardon went.

"That's what's up King. You know I can go for all that and it's no doubt in my mind that anything is funny about your release," he said while looking pops in the eyes. "Still, I was taught by you homie. Your appearance on my steps on your second day home almost makes me want to get my gun."

My pops pointed to the envelope in his hand and passed it over to Bruh. He asked him to skim the contents and tell us what he thought. While Bruh read, my pops motioned for me to join him outside on the porch.

Out there, my pop's eyes scanned the streets as if looking for our tail. He was paranoid. I had a feeling that was the reason that we came outside in the cold. Either he thought yo's house was bugged or he wanted to check for the tail. I stepped off the porch for a better look at the streets myself. I didn't see anything suspicious and returned back to the porch. Bruh came out at that moment with a puzzled look on his face.

"The gun that they retrieved was the same gun that was supposed to be at the bottom of the harbor," my pops stated. "That's the same gun that I used on Bo Pete's bitch ass. If you remember, after that hit, me, you, and T.O. all went to Sallie Mae's joint to regroup. I told you to get rid of that…"

"But T.O. volunteered," Bruh said cutting him off. "I remember like it was yesterday. He said something about going over to that bitch Kristy's house and that he would get rid of the gun on the way."

My pops nodded and smiled. He and Bruh were on the same page. I exhaled quietly. I really didn't know what this whole meeting was about. For all I knew, shit could've gotten ugly real quick. My pops reached for the papers and started to point out some other things. I leaned over and checked out the court documents with them.

"Those motherfuckers charged me with murder, racketeering, money laundering and a bunch of other shit. They had good information too. It was inside info and these papers convinced me who the snitch was."

My pops paused for effect. Bruh stood and started to pace. He wanted to say something but no words came out of his mouth. He went into the house and returned with the bottle. He started to swig from it.

"I could've beaten the whole case. I lie to you not. It wasn't until fifteen days before trial that the state's attorney turned over this paperwork. After reading this shit, I knew who C/I 0543325 was and knew that I couldn't beat the rap. I had to plea."

Bruh took a big swallow from the bottle; started mumbling to himself. He asked my pops why he held this info from him for twenty years. Better yet, he wanted to know why he let him sit under T.O. for so long.

I looked at yo. He was not bullshitting. The love that he had for pops was evident in his eyes.

The realization that he was dealing with a snitch had him really in his feelings.

"Really, I can't believe that you stayed under him for so long. I kept tabs on both of you from word of mouth. My source told me that you two were inseparable. What I can't figure out is how you let him gain so much while you sat in the shadow?"

Bruh shook his head and said that he didn't want the heat that T.O. had. He stated that he was richer now than he ever dreamed he could be and could walk away at any time.

Pop nodded his head and brushed a little lint off his jacket like a boss. I wanted to know how he planned to handle this situation. Finally he asked Bruh where they should go from here.

Bruh hunched his shoulders. He gave me a look and finally snapped his fingers.

"You're Rah's cousin. I knew I had seen you somewhere before." A frightened look came over his face. "Fuck me crazy. This is yours and Gloria's boy. That means Rah is Glo's sister's boy. How didn't I put this all together I don't know."

He became quiet. Finally he got up and came back with his cellular dialing frantically. I gave pops a look. He nodded to let me know it was all good.

"Don't tell that motherfucker that I'm out," pops warned.

Bruh held up a finger for silence. He said that he wasn't calling T.O. He stopped talking, cursed out loud and then started dialing again. As he texted, he started to explain.

"T.O. has a hit man. Actually it's a hit woman and this bitch is vicious. I have to call her," he pointed a finger at me. "Your life is in danger."

I started to question this but then it hit me. A bitch...Rah was gunned down by a bitch. I asked him to tell me more about the hit woman.

"She's a white woman. The broad is international. In fact, she's one of the best. You wouldn't have seen her coming."

Pops didn't let him continue. In a flash, he whipped out his .38 and had it to Bruh's head. He asked him how he could let T.O. put a hit out on his son. Murder was in his eyes.

"I didn't know man. I swear...This is my first time meeting your son man!" He paused to get his thoughts together. "Sure, I knew that you and Glo had kids but I never knew that Rah and Prince were your family."

I reached for my pop's arm. For some reason, I believed Bruh. I told him that he should at least listen to all that Bruh had to say. While all that was taking place, Bruh's cellular rang in his hand. It was a text message. He read it and then showed it to pops. The message read, 'Cancel it? Which one?

Both???' Bruh started to respond but pops stopped him.

"I want that bitch too. Can you set her up," pops asked.

Bruh stopped texting. He told pops that he had never actually met the bitch personally. His job had basically been to relay messages and transfer money.

"Transfer money," pops asked.

"Yeah, you know, after the job is done."

Pops digested that info. After a minute or two he gave Bruh permission to cancel the hits. We sat around in silence and waited for a confirmation. Her message came through a while later. She asked to get paid. Bruh hesitated.

"Shit, I forgot that the bitch still gets paid." He got up to get his laptop. Pops and I stood over his shoulder as he worked. I whistled once I saw the money that was being transferred into her account. I commented on how expensive she was.

"Yeah, she is expensive, but she's one of the best. Shorty is like some shit out of a book. You can only read about the shit that she does."

After the money was confirmed, shorty hit right back telling us to have a nice day. I don't know if pops realized it or not but it was no doubt in my mind that shorty was probably the same tail that we had spotted earlier. Just the thought of how close death was made me shiver.

"Alright, with that business settled, we can concentrate on how we're gonna handle this fuck nigga," pops said as he started to pace.

Bruh stepped in then. He told pops that old boy wouldn't be a problem for anyone after he got finished with him. Pops studied yo for a minute, probably wondering if he could still trust him. After a moment, he pointed a finger at him and grinned.

"Listen up I'm heading out of town to chill with the family for a minute. Handle this for your boy while I'm gone and I'll have something special for you upon my return."

* * * * *

(Princess)

"So what do you think," I asked Fire.

We were seated at a Denny's picking at the remains of a breakfast that had started over an hour ago. In that time, I had basically taxi cab confessed about me and the person that I am.

For starters, we had made it out of my crib earlier without a confrontation, which was a good thing because shit could have easily gone south. To my surprise, Hood took the high road and bowed out gracefully. I made a mental note to call him in the future to try and explain my position better.

"Wow," Fire said as he shook his head. "You just said a mouth full."

Fresh

I couldn't blame him for his reaction. Something about yo had me off balance. I had just brought him up to speed on who I was and what he was dealing with. And just to show him that I was really an extraordinary bitch and not just after his money or status, I whipped out my I-phone and accessed my account for him to see.

"So as you can see, I believe in honesty. I'm sorry for that awkward position I had you in earlier," I said.

A waiter came over and cleared away our trash. We got up to leave. In the Bentley, I retrieved my stash of diesel and let him roll up.

"So you say that your pops used to run this city," he asked as I maneuvered through the town. I was headed for the Galleria mall to pick up Quita a few birthday gifts.

"That's the story I've been whispered since I was a little girl," I confessed.

He nodded and said that one person running a city was hard to believe. He added that he knew first hand that Baltimore is rumored to be one of the roughest cities in the United States. I told him that he watched too much of the Wire and we both got a good laugh out of that one.

"Are we gonna swing through and meet pops today," Fire asked.

"We may be able to pull that off," I replied before explaining that my pops had proposed last night and that the family was supposed to board a flight to Vegas tonight.

"Man, that's what's up," Fire stated.

"Yeah, they're gonna do their thing and then go off to Aspen to honeymoon. After that, we all supposed to meet in Florida to vacation together," I informed while taking the blunt that he offered. "My mom rented a crib down there on Star Island right next to Diddy's joint."

He whistled and told me that all that sounded nice and expensive. He added that he had been to Diddy's crib on the island and that the shit was off the chain; said that he had worked with yo on his 'Press Play' album.

I decided to make my pitch and told him that I was gonna be some kind of lonely down in Florida and that he was welcome to join me down there.

"I might just can do that," he nodded. "I got to check my schedule first. I know I'm gonna be in Puerto Rico over the holidays, but after that, I might be free."

I knew he had a baby's mother and two kids down in Puerto Rico. I saw pictures on the wall while at his crib. His extended family didn't intimidate me though.

"Whatever is clever, you know. Let me know and I'll even pick up the bill," I offered while passing the blunt his way. "You know, fly down on a G-5 and take you shopping at Gucci. I can show you a good time like you did me."

He burst out laughing and told me that he was definitely gonna take me up on my offer because he loved himself some Gucci.

* * * * *

(Gloria)

I was dictating a letter to a client when I got the call that the verdict was back. I glanced at the clock. It was seventeen after three. That meant the jury had only deliberated five hours. The short deliberation could only mean a guilty verdict and that pissed me off. The competitor in me can't stand to lose.

At the same time, I felt a jolt of excitement. No matter what the outcome was, I would still be able to leave and go home to King. It's fucked up that I feel this way, but I rationalized that my client is stupid anyway and should have taken the probation that was offered to him. Whatever the case, I headed to the restroom real quick to refresh my makeup.

When I stepped out into my secretary's office, she was busy tipping the delivery guy for a beautiful arrangement of roses. Roses are my favorite too. I went over to get a sniff. I asked Laura who they were from. She handed me the card.

'Might as well get used to them; they'll be coming your way a lot now that I'm home. Have a good day and good luck with the verdict; love, King.'

I grinned like a Cheshire cat. That man never ceased to amaze me. I felt a shiver of anticipation run down my spine as I thought of a repeat performance of last night going down as soon as I stepped in the house. Laura cleared her throat and pointed at the door to remind me that I had court.

"Just a while longer and you can thank him in person," she grinned with a knowing smile while handing me a piece of paper. "You have three suites booked at Caesar's. The jet will be on standby tonight so you can board at any time."

I asked if everything was arranged in Aspen. She confirmed that the refrigerator was stocked with food, honey and whipped cream in case I felt the need to get a little freaky. I thanked her with a wink and headed for the elevator.

* * * * *

(T.O.)

"Does that feel good to you Poppy," Chyna asked.

I was stretched out on my bed while Chyna sat astraddle me massaging the kinks and tension out of my shoulder. I had a lot of shit on my mind. I had gotten an emergency call from my insurance company informing me that my biggest dealership had been vandalized. Apparently, Rah's people were desperate and since they couldn't pinpoint my location, they attacked my business. According to my insurance agent, someone had shot up every car on the lot. Everything was totaled and beyond repair.

That was definitely a bitch move on his part, but two could play those games. I had plans to get the warehouse where they kept all that construction equipment vandalized and I was gonna get that club his cousin opened in D.C. shut down. Not only that, but I planned to push Bonnie even harder to complete those hits.

I had been calling Bruh's phone all day and wasn't getting an answer. That was real unusual on his part. It could only be two reasons why his phone could be turned off and I dreaded both of them. The first was that he could be somewhere dead. Maybe Rah's goons had somehow gotten to him. The second explanation was that maybe the feds had gotten to him. That could be even worse than his death. Even though Bruh had zero tolerance for rats, I still was convinced that the feds had ways of abstracting certain info from him that could lead to my demise.

After I couldn't get in touch with him, I went on the internet to watch the city's news and read the paper. It was in the local and state section of The Sun that I read my third and biggest fear. The article read…

'Baltimore Drug Dealer Pardoned' by Adrian Allen.

After twenty years of incarceration, Bryce Orlando Williams, also known as King, was released from the Bureau of Prisons in Petersburg, Virginia today. A spokesperson for the white house confirmed that Mr. Williams and six others were being granted a full pardon. The report failed to go into detail of the exact reasons these men were released. Mr. Williams, a Baltimore native was sentenced…

My former road dog and best friend was free. How he got out, I have no idea. I was more worried if he knew that I was C/I 0543325; and if he did, what to expect from him. In fact, I knew that he had to know that I was the informant who sent him away. He was too smart not to know. He had basically confirmed that after my visits were denied and my money orders were returned to me.

His release made me want to find Bruh even more. Plans were starting to change. Rah and Prince could wait. I needed to put Bonnie on his ass first and foremost. Shit, it would be better to get him and his family together. Headlights approaching and the sound of tires on the gravel alerted me that someone was coming. I almost knocked Chyna to the floor as I got up to see who it was.

"Damn, daddy; are you trying to break a bitch neck," she whined.

I noticed my Maybach approaching when I peeked out the window. I instantly slipped into some pajama bottoms and headed to greet him.

"Nigga, you had me worried for a second. What in the hell is wrong with your phone," I asked as I let him into my study.

He gave me a lame excuse about dropping in the toilet and not having time to replace it yet. I knew very little about cellular phones myself and didn't think to question him further. I did ask him why he hadn't contacted me this evening.

"I just told you that my phone's fucked up and you wouldn't believe that I don't know your number by heart. I went by the dealership to get it from Kristy and whole place was taped off. That's why I'm here now."

I let him know that I was already aware of that situation and we had more pressing issues to deal with. I went over to my computer and pulled the article on King. After reading it, he started to smile.

"He's out? King's out," he asked as if he didn't just read the fucking article for himself. I got up and went to pour us both a drink. "That's what's up. I'll hunt him down tomorrow…"

I cut him off and told him that he may need to kill King's ass when he found him. He gave me a puzzled look. I nodded.

"He's got to go," I affirmed.

"What the fuck…I mean, what's up?"

"What's up is that Bonnie is out there hunting his son as we speak my nigga."

He raised his eyebrow so I gave him the full rundown. I told him that Rah's cousin, the pretty boy with the black Bentley was King's son. I could tell that he was really lost now so I explained even further. When I finished, I told him that things had gone too far to pull out now. I iterated that the best thing for everyone would be for King, his son and nephew to end up in a ditch somewhere, soon.

"T.O. man, this is King that we're talking about. He understands these streets like none other. If anything…"

I let him ramble on while I went to top off our drinks. I heard footsteps approaching and called Chyna into the room. She came in wearing only a short robe that was opened for all to see her goodies. She made no move to cover up either. Bruh had seen it all at the club before anyway. She nodded at Bruh. I told her to bring more ice from the kitchen for me.

"Listen to me good Bruh. I know what I'm about to do. The question is, are you with me or…"

Fresh

I had to stop in my tracks because Bruh had unveiled a small revolver from his inside coat pocket and had it pointed at me. Murder was in his eyes.

"What the fuck man," I questioned.

"Shut the fuck up, you rat bitch!" He hissed between gritted teeth. "If anyone got to go it's your bitch ass."

I was completely caught off guard. He had called me a rat which led me to believe that he knew of all my treachery that I had pulled years ago or recently. Whatever the case, I wasn't a dead man yet and intended to keep it that way.

"Now Bruh, I don't know what the hell is going on or what in the hell you done heard, but..." I stopped mid-sentence. I didn't want to tell on myself.

"Oh nigga, you know what the hell is going on. King came by earlier to see me. He brought his court papers with him. Nigga you're a rat, point blank, period."

Before, he was calm. Now, he was on his feet. Never did he raise his voice. I could hear Chyna in the distance moving around the kitchen. I had to alert her of the danger. It was my only chance. I started to talk loud.

"Nigga fuck that nigga King. Why the fuck ain't that nigga here handling his own business. And you, after all I've done for your ass and this..."

That was as far as I got. He pointed the gun and fired. The bullet hit me in the stomach. My insides were on fire. Seeing that blood seep from between my fingers made my bladder burst. I felt hot liquid running down my leg. I could hear Chyna's heels clopping as she made her way towards us. I wanted to yell for her to get help but no words came out when I opened my mouth.

Bruh had maneuvered himself near the door. She dropped the ice bucket when she saw me and opened her mouth to scream. No words came out. Bruh put one in her head. She was dead before she hit the floor.

"Oh shit," I yelled at the sight of her brains splattered on the wall behind her.

Bruh started back in my direction. On the way, he picked up his drink and drained it. When it was empty, he put the whole glass in his pocket. I watched as he pulled a handkerchief from his pocket and started wiping down shit that he may have touched. It was then that I knew I was gonna die. I coughed up some blood.

"Don't do this man. I...I did it for us man!" I started to bawl like a baby. He asked me exactly what did I do for us. At least I had him talking. I started to choose my words wisely.

"I got popped on 95. King had sent me to VA to cop some shit from them New York niggas, but the police pulled me." I coughed and tried to get it together. "Once they found out who I was, the feds came immediately. They laid out all this info that they had on us; me, you, King, Jr. Reid and Scoot. They had us all down bad, but they mainly wanted King. They told me that they would release me and give us all amnesty if I agreed to roll over on King."

"And you didn't hesitate did you? I know you nigga," he said as he shook his head and pointed the gun at me again.

I told him that any of us probably would have done what I did had they been in my shoes. I then pointed out what we had all gone to achieve after King got locked. The nigga Scoot had been buried in a gold casket for Christ's sake. I told him that I organized shit better than King could have ever done and that we were all rich from it.

He stared at me for a long moment as if going over in his head what I had just said. I had to keep him talking.

"King was reckless than a motherfucker. Then the bitch Gloria had his nose open…"

"Nigga, you're a rat and that's all to it. It's motherfuckers like you who have the jails and prisons overpopulated. You're weak; a Sammy the Bull type of nigga. King's a stand up dude. You got no balls; no morals. You will sacrifice anyone to save yourself."

He raised the gun and fired. The first bullet missed. The second shot grazed my ear. I rolled out of the chair. I was literally holding my ear in place. I decided to play possum. He wasn't going for it though. He came over and kicked me in the face. I coughed up more blood.

"It ain't over bitch. I'm gonna torture your ass slowly," he promised.

I started to protest. I told him that he would have told everything if his back was against the wall. I couldn't believe that I was actually taunting a man with my life in his hands. I was delusional. My taunting made him madder.

"Nigga, I'm a gangster. I live by the code. John Gotti said it best when he said that he would do a thousand years in Marion before he pled guilty. I feel the same way," he shouted before shooting me in the arm.

"Oh shit…please God. Damn," I screamed and started to crawl for my life. "Money…I'll pay you. Get the computer and I'll wire you fifty million right now. Just don't kill me man," I pleaded.

It's true what they say. Money truly is the root of all evil. I had his undivided attention. He looked over at the computer, then back towards me. He lowered the gun; wanted to even smile. Every man has a price. Every nigga wanted money, power and respect. I made another plea for the computer.

Fresh

Just when I thought that I had him, he turned the gun back in my direction.

"Fuck you, you rat ass motherfucker!"

With those words, he pulled the trigger and sent me to my maker.

To Be Continued…

The Family: Money, POWER, Respect II

Coming Soon

Fresh

Book Order Form

To order additional copies of this and all publications from Unique Literature Publications, please completely fill out the form below and mail to the address provided along with check or money order

Name: _____

Address: _____

_____

Email: _____

Telephone: _____

Number of Copies: _____

Send this order form to:
Unique Literature Publications
C/O Lorenzo King
417 Gulley St.
Goldsboro, NC 27530
To order via PayPal email:
Renzoking33@gmail.com or call (336) 709-2080
for more information.

Book Order Form

To order additional copies of this and all publications from Unique Literature Publications, please completely fill out the form below and mail to the address provided along with check or money order

Name: _____

Address: _____

_____

Email: _____

Telephone: _____

Number of Copies: _____

Send this order form to:
Unique Literature Publications
C/O Lorenzo King
417 Gulley St.
Goldsboro, NC 27530
To order via PayPal email:
Renzoking33@gmail.com or call (336) 709-2080
for more information.

The Family: MONEY, Power, Respect

www.ingramcontent.com/pod-product-compliance
Lightning Source LLC
Chambersburg PA
CBHW062155270326
41930CB00009B/1545